A
JOURNEY
OF
THE HEART

ALAN LEWIS

A JOURNEY OF THE HEART

EXPLORATIONS INTO
THE EXPERIENCE
OF PRAYER

AN ALBATROSS BOOK

© Alan Lewis 1995

Published in Australia and New Zealand by
Albatross Books Pty Ltd
PO Box 320, Sutherland
NSW 2232, Australia
in the United States of America by
Albatross Books
PO Box 131, Claremont
CA 91711, USA
and in the United Kingdom by
Lion Publishing plc
Peter's Way, Sandy Lane West
Oxford OX4 5HG, England

First edition 1995

National Library of Australia
Cataloguing-in-Publication data

Lewis, Alan (Alan Edgar)
A Journey of the Heart

ISBN 0 7324 1045 2

1. Prayer — Christianity. I. Title

248.32

Cover photograph: John Waterhouse
Printed and bound in Australia by Griffin Paperbacks, Netley, SA

Contents

*This is for Peter Balmer
and the people of Christ Church,
Geelong*

Introduction

A PLACE FOR WONDERFUL FOOD at reasonable prices, off-beat clothes, bookshops and people-watching is Brunswick Street in the inner Melbourne street of Fitzroy. One of the bookshops has a substantial section on what might best be described as 'New Age' writing. It seems to specialise in such things as Zen meditation, Celtic mythology, eco-feminism, neo-Paganism, after-death experiences, the healing properties of crystals and aromatherapy. This section of the shop is quite popular, particularly among young people, and looking through what is currently in vogue has become a particular fascination for me.

On one such visit, a couple browsing on the other side of the book table struck up a conversation. The young woman asked me whether I was into American

Indian religion. When I inquired why she asked, she pointed to a ring I was wearing, commenting that it was very much like what a Navaho religious leader or shaman might wear. The ring consisted of a piece of veined turquoise set into silver. It was a gift from an American friend with whom I had been studying the Christian tradition of spiritual direction. She told me that among some of the native peoples of my friend's country, the turquoise was the sign of the inner wisdom that came from the heavens and was worn by their spiritual guides. Her hope was that I might strive to become what it represented and grow in wisdom as a 'soul friend' to others on their spiritual pilgrimage. I haven't coped all that well with the implications of this gesture and often self-consciousness has led me to leave the ring in a drawer.

The couple introduced themselves as Shelley and Doug. I briefly related to them the story of the gift, which led to an opportunity for numerous cups of coffee in a nearby shop. I listened to Shelley talk at length about shamanism and American Indian spirituality, and what she had tried to understand about the world view of Australia's indigenous people. Her spiritual search had led her away from the nominal Christianity of her family. They had not really attended any church apart from being guests at occasional rites of passage. Having absorbed family attitudes, she did not believe that Christianity had anything to offer except stern moralism and dull ceremonies.

After a while, Shelley and Doug began to ask me about my own spirituality, and expressed surprise that there was such a long and rich tradition of prayer and meditation in 'mainline' Christianity — and, further, that I could still be a Christian, given what they perceived to be the irrelevance of Western institutional religion, particularly in Australia. I have ceased to be amazed that so many people of integrity genuinely seem to hold to such an opinion. They wanted to talk some more and, as the weeks went by, became part of a rather loose circle who met to debate and share insights about the 'inner journey'.

A lot of this kind of sharing has coloured the writing of this book. Coupled with this is my own encounter with God which, over years, has resulted in all kinds of faltering responses. The main theme rests on the belief that prayer is that dialogue which is created in the human heart in response to the touch of Love. It involves the experience of the loving invitation to relationship which emanates from one at the heart of the universe I have called 'the Cosmic Lover' — the one whom Christians identify as God.

I am continually fascinated by the God who has

drawn me further into relationship. The insights of
Lady Julian of Norwich, the fourteenth-century
English mystic who saw God as the ground of all
her prayer, find an echo in my own experience.
After pondering the meaning of this relationship
over many years, she came to understand:

> . . .that love is our Lord's meaning. And I saw very
> certainly in this and in everything that before God made
> us he loved us, which love was never abated and never
> will be. And in this love he has done all his works, and
> in this love he has made all things profitable to us, and in
> this love our life is everlasting. In our creation, we had
> beginning, but the love in which he created us was in him
> from without beginning. In this love, we have our
> beginning and all this shall we see in God without end.[1]

Two more things have enriched my own experience and understanding of the love of God and the
life of prayer: the daunting task of teaching others,
and the even more awesome responsibility of acting
as a 'soul friend' to a small group of people on their
spiritual journey. The more I have experienced
these things, the more I know I am still a beginner
in the way of prayer. It was somewhat of a surprise
that Ken Goodlet of Albatross Books should approach me to write this book. I am grateful for his
encouragement and guidance — and for the learning which has come from the attempts to write.

I have found a greater freedom to express myself and share my experiences using the literary form of 'letters to Peter'. While the names and some places are largely fictitious, the characters and the conversations come from those with whom I have had the privilege of sharing much of my life. Much has been gained from conversations over meals as well as in the lively dialogue of workshop and seminar. As people have tried to grapple with some of the big issues which cannot be avoided when thinking about what goes on when 'prayer has been valid',[2] so I have also grown in my own understanding of what I experience as I grow in relationship with God. Thus, I am grateful to those who have been part of this process over the years and so contributed indirectly to the shape of this book.

The first 'letter to Peter' endeavours to establish something of the way Christians think about God and how this relates to the experience of prayer. God is presented as the Cosmic Lover at the heart of the universe who brings all things into being for relationship with God. God seeks intimacy with us. Prayer is the response we make to the one who courts us. In the second letter, the environment that fosters a wholesome relationship with the Cosmic Lover is considered. The connecting point between the human and the divine is established and the importance of time, solitude and silence are examined.

The third letter takes this further, raising such matters as the value of bodily stillness, ways of quietening the mind, methods which assist us to focus and concentrate, and the similarities and differences which set apart a Christian approach to prayer from other forms of meditation. In the fourth letter, I share my own adaptation of an ancient way of prayer using the Bible known as '*lectio divina*'. In this letter, other methods of using the Bible in prayer are considered as well as some exploration of the use of 'active imagination'. The fifth letter looks at the prayer for others — the invitation to love which we call 'intercession'. It examines some of the images of God which may need to be discarded and the paradoxes which seeking to change the world raises.

Christians do not live their relationship with the Cosmic Lover in isolation. The sixth letter explores something of what it means to pray within the Christian community, and I share something of what that encounter has meant to me in my own journey in the life of prayer. Some religious traditions major on the importance of the 'guru' or spiritual guide. Letter seven looks at the Christian tradition of teachers and guides in the life of prayer, and I share something of my own experience of the ministry of 'soul friends'.

The eighth letter examines the false dichotomy

which sets the physical against the spiritual or the body against the spirit. It seeks to examine the implications of the Christian belief about Jesus 'becoming flesh' on the way we look at creation — the world and our own bodies. Letter nine is a personal reflection on the Christian experience of fasting in relation to prayer. The tenth letter looks at the experience sometimes called 'the dark night of the soul', when the Cosmic Lover seems to abandon us and our experience of prayer appears to dry up.

Finally, I wish to record my gratitude to Barry Smith, Lyn O'Connor and Robin LaTrobe, companions on the way, who have made encouraging and wise suggestions during the period of writing. Likewise, those who attended the Exploration into Prayer seminars at Christ Church, Geelong during 1993. These people, in sharing their own encounters with the Cosmic Lover in the way of prayer, have become a valued source of wisdom and encouragement.

1

The Cosmic Lover at the heart of the universe

Dear Peter,

The evening we shared last night was one of those rare combinations of superlative food, company and conversation. David and Jane are great hosts and I admire the way they include so many in the warmth of their friendship and their home. Drinking excellent coffee sitting around a roaring fire is not the ambience I usually associate with a lively discussion about the Christian understanding of God and the experience of prayer.

I appreciated your honesty during the evening and your request to put some of my thoughts and experiences on paper so that you could give them a little more consideration. I am more than happy to do so and, having had many hours debating with students over the years, I revel in the experience of grappling with such things. There is no need to apologise for what you mistakenly perceive as a burden.

I agree that, at first sight, prayer might seem to be a rather stupid business. As you pointed out last night, assuming that there is a God and that there is some divine interest in what some individual human being wants, there appear to be ridiculous notions associated with prayer. As you said, if God is omniscient — if God knows all things — some praying apparently implies the opposite. God does *not*-know what is going on — or perhaps is not paying attention and needs to be reminded.

You rightly indicated that Christians claim that God is love, and yet prayer seems to imply that God is the opposite — uncaring, distant, lazy, capricious, or has to be cajoled or pleaded with to attend to the matters expressed in prayer. I think we all shared your discomfort with a Christian community which has pastors in Germany asking the blessing of God on bombs destined for England during World War II, and English chaplains praying for the success of the bombing of German cities. We could smile at your sympathy for God faced with a dilemma when in the same area some people pray for rain for the growth of their crops and others pray for sunshine because they are about to commence holidays.

I have the same concerns which you expressed last night, but they do not lead me to abandon the practice of prayer. As you have asked for 'something in writing', I will attempt to share with you how I try to deal with these issues. First, however, I need to explain the reason for my prayer. This will involve some journeying into Christian theology, so I look forward to some more lively discussion when next we meet.

While there are certain beliefs which are common to most Christians, what I share is coloured by my experience. Just as no two people love each other in identical ways, no two people have an identical experience of the journey of prayer.

Please keep in mind, Peter, that I write as a male, with a particular temperament and upbringing. I am an Australian of Anglo-Celtic ancestry and from a particular experience of the Christian community. That will give my writing a particular shape and texture.

A way of thinking about God

Any attempt to comprehend the Christian experience of prayer must begin with what we understand about God. Here we encounter some problems to do with language. Because we are considering relationship, we are limited to language normally applied to humans — anthropomorphic language.

Traditionally, God is described in masculine terms as if 'he' were male. God is not male — nor is God female. In the first book of the Bible, humankind is described as having been created male *and* female, in the image of God. Now if I use masculine pronouns in my speaking about God, I am reverting to my conditioning in the Christian community of which I am part. Likewise, if I write of God having a 'heart' or 'hands', I do not mean it literally. I am using metaphor.

At the heart of Christian thinking is the notion of God as Trinity. Given our dinner conversation last evening, I know that you are familiar with the writings of Carl Jung. I have found his insights very helpful as I have tried to understand the complexities of the spiritual journey. Jung was the author of the term 'collective unconscious' — containing 'the whole spiritual heritage of mankind's evolution, born anew in the brain structure of every individual'[1] and the 'archetype', referring to the contents of the collective unconscious. He has demonstrated how the 'trinity' motif has parallels in the religious experience of many pre-Christian belief systems — among the Celts, the Babylonians, the Egyptians and the Greeks in particular.[2]

As a Christian, I find this fascinating. It leads me to ponder whether the 'truth' about God is already imprinted within us. Jung in this statement appears to be claiming this: 'The Trinity is an archetype whose dominating power not only fosters spiritual development but may, on occasion, actually enforce it.'[3] As we enter into relationship with God, there is an inner 'familiarity' which makes us a bit more comfortable with what is essentially beyond our comprehension. Perhaps this may have something to do with what the Bible means in stating that humankind is created in the image of God.

Let me first present the big picture, the background of the vast canvas on which we shall paint the detail: Christians believe that God is a Trinity — manifested in the Father, the Son and the Holy Spirit, three and yet *one* God. Also, despite what might seem to shout the opposite, God is Love. Love is not static. In order to exist, it must always be expressed, pouring itself out to another, always giving of itself. So, within the Trinity, there is a constant flow of self-giving, unconditional love, each person delighting in receiving and giving in an ecstasy of being one with the other.

God's love cannot be contained within God's being. In centrifugal energy, it bursts forth in the creation of the cosmos. All that exists is the result of the love of God and comes into being for relationship with God.

This is particularly so of humankind. God creates us in order that we might share in the life and love of the Trinity. That is our destiny, the ultimate purpose of our being — to know and enjoy an intimate friendship with God, to know him 'heart to heart'. Not entering into the fullness of our destiny brings a deep restlessness, a sense of yearning.

It was Augustine of Hippo Regius, that passionate scholar who became a leader among Christians in North Africa in the fifth century and subsequently influenced a great deal of Western Christian thinking, who maintained that God made us for himself and that we experience an inner restlessness until we find that rest in God.

Francis Thompson, the English poet of the Victorian era and one-time opium addict, writes of this in *The Hound of Heaven*. He expresses this inner restlessness throughout his poem in the intense imagery of the fugitive constantly pursued, who in the end finds rest in the gentle acceptance of the God whose hand is 'outstretched caressingly':

Ah, fondest, blindest, weakest,
I am He Whom thou seekest!
Thou dravest love from thee, who dravest Me.[4]

This illustrates in some way the experience of many that, just as God's creative energies have a centrifugal flow, so God's love has a centripetal movement constantly drawing us. Unconditional Love at the heart of the universe unwaveringly seeks the response of love from all of humankind. It leads the human heart into a constant search for the One who draws, courts, lures and — dare I use the term — seduces us!

I do not want to suggest that in prayer we have a permanent end to that inner restlessness. The seventeenth-century English poet John Donne, having sought in the love of another the fulfilment of the inner journey, finds after the death of the lover a quenching of his inner thirst in relationship with God. Yet having found the source, he still experiences the lack of durable satisfaction which drives him on in pursuit of the divine relationship.

In the imagery of illness, he describes it thus:

But though I have found thee,
and thou my thirst hast fed,
A holy thirsty dropsy melts mee yett.[5]

A way of thinking about prayer

Given last night's conversation, Peter, I think at this point you would be somewhat exasperated and about to demand what all this has to do with prayer. Frankly, everything!

I equate prayer with love. Prayer is that expression of love which is constantly flowing in the being of God, in the heart of the Trinity. It flows out from God into the cosmos and flows back to God in response from the whole creation.

While prayer for me might be experienced as something personal and intimate, it is never private. It is part of that pulse of love which permeates the whole universe. To use the words which have for many centuries been part of the liturgy of the Christian community to which I belong, prayer is 'with angels and archangels and all the company of heaven'.[6] It is something cosmic which spans all time and is beyond time. I join in something which is already going on and never ceases. This, I believe, also involves not only the response of humankind and what we term as 'the whole company of heaven', but all of creation.

In a delightful insight, Bonaventure writes about Francis of Assisi:

> One time when Francis was walking with another friar in the Venetian marshes, they came upon a huge flock of birds singing among the reeds. When he saw them, the saint said to his companion, 'Our sisters the birds are praising their Creator. We will go in among them and sing God's praise, chanting the divine office.'
>
> They went in among the birds which remained where they were, so that the friars could not hear themselves saying the office, they were making so much noise. Eventually, the saint turned to them and said, 'My sisters,

stop singing until we have given God the praise to which he has the right.' The birds were silent immediately. . .[7]

Well might this be the stuff of pious legend and poetry, but it is the affirmation that the whole of the creation is involved in prayer. Francis was firmly convinced that the created order, both animate and inanimate, came from the same divine source. As such, he was part of a family which embraced them. He called them 'brother' and 'sister', and for him there was no problem in seeing them united in the prayer of praise to the Creator.

The nineteenth-century English poet Gerard Manley Hopkins wrote in a similar vein as he saw the world 'charged with the grandeur of God. It will flame out, like shining from shook foil. . .'[8]

So even what we would term 'inanimate' things, simply by being, are involved in the cosmic prayer which centres in the life of the Trinity. Each Tuesday morning in the public prayers of the Christian community to which I belong, a canticle is used called *A Song of Creation* which calls upon everything imaginable, both animate and inanimate, to 'bless the Lord: sing his praise and exalt him forever'. The list is very long and includes heavens, angels, waters, sun and moon, stars, rain and dew, winds, fire and heat, summer and winter, dews and frosts, ice and snow, lightning and clouds, mountains and hills, green things, springs, seas and rivers, whales, birds, beasts and cattle, priests, servants, those of upright spirit, the holy and upright in heart.[9]

I believe that this is more than metaphor and poetry, for the universe is not merely a 'system': it is the progeny of the love of the Trinity, part of the endless cosmic hymn. It is this conviction which leads me to stand with those who are passionately concerned about how we treat the earth and its resources — but that is not the concern of the moment.

Thankyou for suggesting that we meet next week for a long lunch to talk further. I have a favourite cafe in Bridge Road which does incredible things with focaccia, has some of the best coffee the city has to offer and is now totally 'smoke-free'. The staff have never expressed any desire to hurry customers along, so I think you'll be impressed with the place.

See you Thursday!

Alan

2

Considerations that foster a wholesome prayer life

Dear Peter,

I'm glad you found the 'Windmill' to your liking. Not only is the food good but, if you're into people-watching, there are some fascinating customers. The regular use of the place for exhibitions of paintings brings students and staff from the local college and, through Jacqui and Owen, I've been introduced to a few budding actors and musicians. I guess it is what my aunt would disapprovingly describe as 'bohemian'.

I did not expect that a long lunch would end up taking five hours! My mind is still pondering the many issues you raised — God, the church, plurality of religious expression, 'New Age' spiritualities, meditation techniques, human sexuality, the environment. . . and if we were both mad enough, we could possibly attempt a few more long lunches to explore the implications a little further. The immediate matter, however, is to fulfil your renewed request to put on paper a few more thoughts about a Christian experience of prayer for further reference.

First, let us assume the broad canvas suggested in my last letter, focussing on the Trinity of Love who, in centrifugal energy, brings into being the whole cosmos and, in similar centripetal attraction, lures and courts it into relationship. Yesterday, you asked how this is made concrete for us. Again, this will involve a little journey into some specifically Christian thinking.

In the First Epistle of John, we read:

> God's love for us was revealed
> when God sent into the world his only Son
> so that we could have life through him;
> this is the love I mean:
> not our love for God,
> but God's love for us when he sent his Son
> to be the sacrifice that takes our sins away.[1]

Christians believe that God came into the world in Jesus Christ. We call it 'incarnation' — God assuming human flesh and sharing in *all* of our humanity. In the birth, life, teaching, death and resurrection of Jesus, the unconditional love of the

Trinity is demonstrated. Uniquely in Jesus, we have a tangible experience of the love of God and it is in and through him that Christian prayer is grounded.

Recognise the uniqueness of Jesus

I realise that to make a claim about the uniqueness of Jesus is to leave myself open to accusations of spiritual arrogance and religious bigotry. In striving for a multicultural society, we do not enthusiastically encourage any religious system claiming to be superior to any other, even if that religion happens to have been central in the dominant culture in recent years.

I am not meaning to be paternalistic when I say that the spiritualities of other religions lead many to an authentic experience of the Living God. The experience of the spiritual journey by many who do not claim to be 'Christian' can teach and enrich many Christians. By lightly dismissing the authenticity of the spiritual experience of other religions, Christians are impoverished.

Ultimately, however, Christians believe that as people genuinely seek truth and reality, their journey must lead them to encounter and experience Jesus. He is the Cosmic Lover at the heart of the universe who draws all into intimate relationship with the Trinity. This is affirmed by the apostle Paul. In his dialogue with the philosophers in Athens, he borrows a phrase from a poem by Epimenides and applies it to Jesus: 'In him we live and move and have our being.'[2] So by implication, the more we are in touch with our true selves in the spiritual journey in response to the attraction of God, the more we are led into intimate encounter with God. I wanted to say this before taking up some of the 'how' issues we discussed yesterday.

Draw on the wisdom of the ages

I remember one of my mentors saying to me early in my spiritual journey that the only way to learn about prayer was to pray. Of course, he was right. It is only in the doing that we truly discover what it is all about. Because prayer is about relationship with God, discussion about schemes and techniques can often be unhelpful and miss the point.

Having said that, there is value in looking at the accumulated wisdom on prayer. The Christian community embraces the total spectrum of humankind, having varying personalities and intellectual and emotional characteristics. Each person has a unique relationship with God and the prayer which characterises that relationship will be coloured by such internal things as temperament or psychological make-up, and external things like the cultural context in which it is lived. There is no one normal or proper way to pray.

So amongst the extensive body of writing on the subject, there could be some that just meets your need.

Give prayer time

It was a most astute observation you made when you suggested that, if prayer as relationship with God were to be taken seriously, it would never develop in any mature way if it were only a 'spare time' affair. Significant human relationships are not built on a five-minute-a-day basis.

I have encountered some Christians who try to survive in a relationship with God on what could be termed the 'Dagwood Bumstead' approach. Do you remember the American comic strip character? He was regularly late for the bus, so there was a rush from bedroom to bus stop, a piece of toast grabbed from the table and a kiss for his wife Blondie standing braced at the door with lips puckered! Sadly, some prayer is like that rushed kiss. Trying to build a relationship with God in the midst of a lifestyle that is marked by a necessity to cram so much into a day is very difficult.

When someone tells me that they do not have time to pray, we look together at what constitutes the activities of a typical day. When values and priorities are considered, time can always be found. The problem is not that time is limited, but that there is no real attraction to the adventure or commitment to the possibilities of building a relationship with God.

Find the point of connection

As I said in my last letter, prayer is that expression of love which is constantly flowing in the being of God. It flows out from God into the cosmos and flows back to God in response from the whole creation. Given that prayer goes on without ceasing, it is right to ask where and how we connect. Such terms as 'within', 'in the heart', 'in the depths of one's being', 'at the centre' are often used to describe an awareness that God is not outside us, but is encountered within us. Some who teach about prayer speak about 'the journey inward', 'standing before God with the mind in the heart' or 'centring'.

I have a preference for the term 'centre', probably because it has more commonly been used by my mentors and seems to fit more comfortably with what I experience as an inner locus of prayer. It is impossible to attempt to identify the 'centre' physically or imaginatively; nevertheless, there is an awareness deep within one's being.

Today, we often speak of the heart as the centre of the deepest affections. In the culture of the first Christians, the Greek word *splanchna* (literally 'bowels') was used figuratively as the source of the deepest emotions. To speak of loving with all one's bowels would, in our setting, seem a little vulgar. Yet talking of the heart in the same way is also somewhat absurd, because the heart and the bowels have specific functions in the body that have little to do with how we generally understand emotions.

Speaking in such a way of these parts of the anatomy are attempts to locate and describe what we experience about the things which move us in the depths of our being. I guess this is another reason why I prefer 'centre', for it is free from things anatomical, which often have other unconnected associations.

There is a focus today on the renewal of an ancient Christian prayer form by the Cistercian monk Basil Pennington. He calls this 'Centering Prayer'.[3] While there may be similarities in the framework of my journey into prayer, I am not following Pennington's approach.

When I use the term 'centring', I am referring to the process of tuning-in to the source of prayer and the place where we experience it happening. The process of inner centring is aided by certain outer environments: solitude and silence. It is vital that we acknowledge the influence of the outside environment on the inner milieu.

Seek out solitude and silence

The Gospel of Matthew records Jesus as saying: 'Whenever you pray, go into your room and shut the door and pray to your Father who is in secret. . .'[4] Jesus was teaching about the dangers of public piety in which those he called hypocrites engaged, just to be seen by others. He commended the small store-room attached to the typical house of his times — the only room provided with a door.

There are many who see in this teaching not just a caution about ostentatious piety, but a basic prin-ciple in the practice of prayer. Jesus is reported in the Gospels as leaving where he was staying in order to find a 'solitary place' in which to pray.[5]

Solitude involves a deliberate movement from things which would hinder or distract the primary purpose of prayer. It may involve physically mov-ing away from sources of distraction, from noise to a place of quiet; from being among people to being alone; from an environment of movement and bus-tle to a place of stillness; from a scene which is ugly to one of beauty and tranquillity; from the constant demands of everyday life to a place where one cannot easily be found.

Some have an ability to establish an inner solitude which enables them truly to be centred despite what goes on around them. They can be in the middle of some external 'storm' and yet find an undistracted focus within, enabling them to be attuned to prayer. This perhaps is true solitude.

The importance of 'place' is allied to our search for solitude but, as I want to talk about that in more detail later, I will only refer to it briefly in this context. Some of my fellow travellers have found it helpful to create a special place for prayer. A lady I met in a class I was teaching some years ago lived in an inner urban terrace house which sported an old lavatory at the back of the property which, more than a century ago, was serviced from a rear lane. The house, now blessed with interior plumbing, had rendered the old loo obsolete. This she had stripped of all fittings, painted and, with rush matting on the floor, a stool, and an icon on the wall, she created a place of solitude for her prayer. If you can cope with an awful pun on Vatican architecture, I'll tell you what she called it: her Cistern Chapel!

I know those who have a special chair or a corner of a room which becomes an oratory — a place of prayer. Others find it helpful to use an open church which is used for personal prayer and thus has a welcoming prayer space. Sadly, this is not all that common. I personally do not find solitude in many churches. They are often full of ecclesiastical clutter or are furnished in what screams at me as bad taste and, instead of creating solitude for my prayer, they encourage latent pyromania!

At this stage of my life, I find solitude more in the 'natural' order rather than in the creations of humankind. So, because of easy access, it is more often on the cliff overlooking the sea, or during a walk in the bush, that I find the necessary solitude for my prayer. When I was in Western Australia, I was regularly able to use a small cave in a spectacular gorge through which flowed the Murchison River. Here, there was great stillness and solitude only occasionally disturbed by a feral goat or small lizard, and an enveloping silence which encouraged communion with God.

Solitude is not an escape from reality, nor is it an end in itself, but it is an essential environment which encourages the journey to the centre where one can become attuned to prayer. The deliberate search for solitude is part of a loving response to the God who, constantly searching for us, draws us into relationship.

If we understand that prayer is continually going on in the being of God — that it is intrinsically God's activity in us and that we need to become attuned to it in the centre of our being — then silence is imperative if we are to hear. As the writer on spirituality, Henri Nouwen says, 'Silence is the way to make solitude a reality.'[6]

The experience of silence often arouses negative feelings. Some of my fellow Christians have expressed fear that they are opening themselves to the activity of evil when they enter the silence. Remembering your expressions of skepticism about personifications of evil, Peter, I hope you will be understanding in my reference to these matters. There is a genuine fear in some about confronting evil and scoffing doesn't help them!

Apart from my own experience, I am helped by something I remember in the teaching of St John of the Cross. John was a great sixteenth-century Spanish mystic who wrote much about the spiritual journey. He strongly believed that no evil was permitted to confuse the one who, in response to the call of God, entered the silence to experience God's love in prayer.

We live at a time when the experience of silence is not common or popular. Those who live in cities would rarely be confronted with the absence of noise. There is always the rumble of the products of our technology in the background both night and day. Our lives are flooded with an epidemic of words wherever we turn. There are those whose radios are never turned off because of what is experienced without them. Muzak has been created so that we will not feel ill at ease in places where silence might increase our levels of stress.

Some years back while living in Geraldton in Western Australia, for solitude and prayer I often went to nearby Ellendale Pool, a place with still water alongside a spectacular cliff. Apart from the birds who nested in the cliff, there was an overwhelming tranquillity which I found very therapeutic, but only in 'off peak' times, because it was frequently visited by people with deafening ghetto blasters who shattered the atmosphere with music from the local radio station. Perhaps the silence of the place made them afraid.

External silence often confronts people with their inner noise. This can often be associated with things which are uncomfortable or even threatening within. Understandably, there is a hasty retreat into a noisy environment. This meeting with the darkness within is a necessary part of the encounter with God.

Two very important things happen when we do not flee from the experience; both involve the breaking of false images. First, there will be the discovery that God is not like what we thought God to be. There are those who look on God as one who rewards and condemns. Perhaps they have been introduced to a perversion of Christianity which preaches a turning to God to escape punishment or secure eternal life. God for them is like the Monty Python foot which is ready to stomp on any who do not toe the line.

This is but one of many caricatures of God which

God will not own. As C.S. Lewis has noted: 'My idea of God is not a divine idea. It has to be shattered time after time.'[7]

In the silence, the God who draws us lovingly into relationship will shatter our false views to embrace the truth about God. This process can often produce a lot of insecurity. Believe it or not, some would rather cling to some revolting parody of God than confront the implications of 'this is not who I am'. Added to this is the realisation shared by C.S. Lewis that this does not happen just once or twice. It is 'time after time'. But then this is what all relationships are about, are they not? The adventure of friendship is one of constant discovery about the other.

Second, there will be the discovery that we are not like we thought we were. To adapt the C.S. Lewis quote to this context: my idea of *myself* is not a divine idea. It has to be shattered time after time. I cannot play a role in the presence of God. I come as I am. I do not have to dress up. I do not have to be perfect. I don't have to carry great layers of false guilt. However, like the layers of an onion, the encounter with God will peel away the concepts of myself which are not authentic. This process can also be painful, but ultimately it is healing and liberating. Confronted with some ugly caricatures of ourselves, the God who draws us into prayer will assure us that 'this is *not* who you are'.

We have often spoken about the wonderful change we have seen in James since he began sharing his life and love with Tricia. So it is when we encounter God in the prayer which is transfiguring love — we change and move towards becoming our true selves.

That will have to do for now. I think that in making a date for lunch at the 'Fisherman's Net' on Saturday week, we may be establishing a tradition. I hope that the proprietors will be as understanding of our propensity for protracted discussions as they were at the 'Windmill'.

Roll on, Saturday!

Alan

3

The preparation of the body and mind for prayer

Dear Peter,

I was delighted that Sue and Pam were with us yesterday at lunch. Having no thought that you would be sharing our discussions with anyone else, I did not know quite what to expect when you telephoned to suggest that they join us. The 'Fisherman's Net' is not used to the clientele who frequent the 'Windmill', so I was not surprised that we were unable to stay on after lunch. When Pam suggested we savour the shelter of the massive Moreton Bay Fig on the foreshore and continue our conversation, it enhanced an exceptional day!

The journey 'to the centre', as I gather you have been finding in your exploration, is not always easy. While they might not seem very profound and even trivial, nevertheless I have found a few things concerning the body in relation to prayer which are helpful.

Cultivating bodily stillness

Physical tension can become a distracting barrier to centring. Perhaps because I am not a gaunt figure, I find that tight clothes and such constrictions as belts and ties can contribute to this and are best avoided. I adopt a posture which assists relaxation, enables necessary attentiveness, but does not induce sleep. Something straight-backed, which keeps the spine perpendicular, is more helpful than a soft lounge chair.

I have two treasures which were gifts from friends on the journey. One is a *zafu* — a cushion often used by those who practise oriental forms of meditation. Once totally relaxed, I can sit comfortably on the *zafu* with my legs folded for long periods of time. The other is a prayer stool which John made from some well-seasoned oak taken during renovations from an old church. This enables me to 'sit' in a kneeling position and, while not as comfortable for me as the *zafu*, it encourages a similar relaxed but attentive state.

If I am outdoors in a solitary place, I still have the same need for an appropriate posture, with the focus on being comfortable and attentive. An old maxim that 'the body shapes the soul' is applicable here.

Trying to 'centre' while lying in the sun on a warm day, or curling up in an enveloping armchair by a blazing fire creates conflicting messages for my brain. While I would not claim that they make connecting with God impossible, I don't associate such situations with the attentiveness which leads me to any robust experience of prayer.

Once I am comfortable and attentive, I then concentrate on my breathing. For most of my life, I had an overwhelming fear whenever I visited a dentist. Noticing the raw panic which had me sweating profusely and almost rigid in her chair, the gentle lady who now cares for my teeth taught me how deep breathing can relax bodily tension and induce a profound inner stillness. I have adapted the method she taught me as part of centring.

I begin by breathing slowly and deeply from the abdomen. Then I focus on stilling my body. Beginning with my feet I move upwards, tensing and relaxing the muscles — calves, thighs, buttocks and stomach, then along the spine and ribs to the neck, hands, elbows, upper arms and shoulders, and then the muscles of the face.

This is not an end in itself. Its purpose is to create a stillness of body that helps the journey to the centre so that we may encounter the loving God who seeks relationship with us.

Keeping body and soul together

Pam made some telling points yesterday in our discussion on the problem of setting the physical against the spiritual. There have been philosophies which have seeped into Christian thinking which claim that the material world is something intrinsically evil, which has to be fought or renounced in order that the spiritual might develop.

There have been periods in Christian history when fostering bodily privation was seen as essential to the practice of prayer. Some who have taught about the spiritual journey have stipulated that growth in relationship with God is unachievable without developing contempt for our bodies and the physical world in general. The resultant asceticism has possibly produced psychologically disturbed people more often than it has people of deep relationship with God.

I'm not sure whether Pam's hilarious story of a medieval eccentric, aptly called 'Lydia the Astounding', who prayed for hours while balancing on a fence, has any basis in history. I wouldn't be surprised if it did. There are many authenticated stories of those who have thrashed themselves, worn hairshirts with metal spikes which dug into the flesh, or endured many ingenious self-imposed ordeals to focus on what was thought to be the superior or more spiritual activity.

It is necessary to question what is obviously unhealthy behaviour.

Christianity at its best shuns anything which pitches the body against the soul. We were created to delight in our bodies, to cherish the healthy pleasure of the senses and to bring them into unity, balance and harmony as we develop in our relationship with God.

Quietening the mind

Sometimes, in my experience, the mind does not reflect the stillness of the body. It continues to rush from thought to thought — distracted, unable to focus — and again becomes an obstacle in the movement of response to the God who draws us into prayer.

I have been helped by a principle taught over the centuries by many teachers about prayer in the Christian tradition. Bustling minds can be given something to do to bring them discipline and assist in entering the silence. You are no doubt familiar with the Hindu term 'mantra' — a word or phrase used in constant repetition as part of meditation. While the term comes from Sanskrit, the method is not uniquely Hindu, as it has been part of the tradition of Christian prayer for at least fifteen hundred years.

It has long been treasured among Eastern

Christians, but lately has begun to be rediscovered in the West. The Christian mantras have been evolved from such sources as significant phrases from the Psalms, short 'one liner' prayers, or a repetition of the name of Jesus.

Paradoxically, they can be considered as both preparations for prayer and part of prayer itself. I seek to coordinate the repetition of my mantra with my breathing, until the upper levels of my mind are stilled and the deeper level becomes focussed in the silence and begins to encounter the prayer that the Spirit of God is praying at the centre of my being.

The mantra which I most commonly use I first encountered during a visit to the ecumenical monastic community in the French village of Taizé. Increasingly, this is becoming a place of pilgrimage for people from all over the world. This is particularly so for thousands of young people — possibly because in a period where they have encountered a spiritual dryness in the church, here they find a lifestyle and spirituality which is clearly authentic or, to use T.S. Eliot's term, a place 'where prayer has been valid'.[1]

In their daily round of communal prayer, the Brothers use simple repetitive prayer songs, which are, in effect, mantras. Because these prayers are sung, they involve more of us. I guess it was this realisation which led to the saying attributed to

Augustine of Hippo Regius: 'The one who sings, prays twice.' In singing them over and over again, they move from the mind into the heart. They focus the mind and, by encouraging centring, lead to the place of prayer.

I commonly use for my mantra a phrase which I first encountered as a Taizé chant: '*O Christe Domine Jesu*', 'O Lord Jesus Christ'. I prefer it in Latin as it has a more sonorous sound and rhythm. If it is appropriate to my place of prayer, and I am not specifically connecting it to my breathing, I sing. It has now become so much part of me that most times the mantra quickly carries me through the distractions which hinder, into a deep stillness and silence where I can pray. If I am further distracted or find my mind wandering where I do not want it to go, I return to the mantra so that I can resume my focus on God.

You asked yesterday about the merits of closing the eyes or using some external object as a focus. The answer lies in what helps us most to be centred on God. Because my surroundings can often become a distraction, I find it more useful to close my eyes. This for me is more conducive to an inner attentiveness. I realise that this has a lot to do with temperament.

Others may need an external focus to assist in centring. These are important if they are a means to bring us to prayer rather than being ends in themselves. Perhaps it is best to look on these as companions to prayer. The use of symbols such as an open Bible, a cross or crucifix, an icon or other piece of religious art, or the lighting of a candle or oil lamp, create sacred space which can encourage focussing on God.

I have had students who became enthused by Carl Jung's writing on symbolism and began to experiment with Christian adaptations of mandalas, which had similar benefits. Nevertheless, I recall one of my mentors offering a wise opinion on these things. It went something like this:

> A little child can become more fascinated with the beautiful paper and ribbon whichsurrounds a gift than with the gift itself. If we become more attached to the things which are meant to point us to God than to God himself, we have little spiritual maturity and are indeed to be pitied.

Praying at the centre

Yesterday, Sue first asked about what happens when the body and mind are stilled and one enters the silence at the centre, and then how this is related to such things as transcendental meditation — TM for short.

What happens at the centre is really up to God. God is the one who creates and draws us into intimate friendship. We cannot manipulate any-thing connected with that encounter. Our task is to respond to God's invitation. That is what all our discussion about solitude and silence has been about. And again, because relationships between lovers are never identical, so no two people will experience God in prayer in the same way. I value two affirma-tions — one from Carl Jung and one from the apostle Paul.

Jung did not go along with the idea that God was 'wholly other'. He considered that such a thing was 'psychologically quite unthinkable'. For him, God was 'one of the soul's deepest and closest intima-cies'.[2] What Jung describes is what I mean by the term 'the centre'. God is not absent, 'in heaven' or 'out there'. God is intimately connected to the core of our being and no-one who genuinely seeks rela-tionship with God will find the search fruitless.

With this I couple what the apostle Paul wrote. We do not know how to pray appropriately, but the Spirit of God prays in us in a way beyond mere words, and that prayer brings us into union with the very mind of God.[3] We can certainly trust that God will be there to nourish the relationship with us. God will lead us whether this involves dialogue, our own verbal responses, or what one of my mentors termed 'pregnant silence'.

I want to follow this up in more detail later.

Focussing on God alone

Sue was right in observing that there are a lot of
similarities between what we discussed yesterday
and what I have come to understand as the meditation technique taught by Maharishi Mahesh Yogi,
known as transcendental meditation. She obviously
has more knowledge of TM than I do, so I hope I am
not being unfair in making comparisons with my
Christian understanding and experience.

I risk showing lack of respect and considerable
superficiality if I try to deal with TM in a few
sentences. Nevertheless, I think both approaches
appear to be based on different principles.

The purpose of practising TM is usually centred
on the results it seeks to achieve — inner tranquillity
and a consequent harmony with the rest of creation.
The purpose of centring prayer is to focus on God
alone, in response to God's invitation to relationship. It may have as an end result some inner peace,
but that is not its purpose.

Instead of using a *mantra* which has an affective
response, the practice of TM involves using one which
is most often bereft of meaning to the one who uses
it. It is to be used constantly throughout the period
of meditation as an end in itself. TM is not a prayer
method and the TM organisation would discourage
it from being adapted as such. Centring has prayer
as its goal and the purpose of the Christian *mantra*

is to lead into the presence of God, or back into it if we have become distracted. It is no longer necessary to continue using it once it has accomplished its goal.

Yesterday, you asked about how Christians relate the Bible to their experience of prayer. Having established something of the basis for my understanding of prayer, I will tackle this in another letter. I'm going to be away for a few days on the Peninsula this week, away from the telephone and the front door bell.

I am looking forward to some beach walks during the afternoons and some fresh fish from one of the boats moored at the jetty at the bottom of the road.

The mornings are for writing! I hope the weather will be kind.

With warmest regards,

Alan

4

The Bible and prayer as nourishment for each other

Dear Peter,

The past few days have been wonderfully therapeutic. The sea has obliged by displaying many of its moods — from its dark grey anger pounding the beach, to a gentle quiet stillness in emerald green allowing a clear view of Melbourne's great towers across the bay.

I have walked a lot, finished reading a new work about the fourteenth-century lady of prayer, Julian of Norwich, tried cooking some new Greek seafood recipes, and caught up on a month of sleep. Above all, I have had some wonderful space for *lectio divina* — some prayerful reading of the Bible — and because you have asked about it, this will be the subject of this letter.

While the Bible is not the only source of the

revelation of the love of God, Christians believe that it is the optimal place for such revelation. There is in the Christian experience an intimate association between Bible and prayer. Our reading and hearing of the scriptures nourishes our prayer and our prayer causes us to return to the scriptures hungering for more. A multi-faceted dialogue is created in the process between the written word, the God whom we discover at the centre, and ourselves.

The pattern I have found most helpful I learned while living with a Christian community in an ancient tithe barn in the English west country. This way has traditionally been associated with the fifth-century father of Western monasticism, Benedict of Nursia. It can be summed up in the four Latin words: *lectio*, reading or hearing the scriptures; *meditatio*, meditating on the scriptures; *oratio*, responding to the scriptures in prayer; and *contemplatio*, resting in the scriptures in contemplation.

Reading or hearing the scriptures to engender prayer (*lectio*)

There are different kinds of Bible reading. There is reading to bring knowledge. This involves knowing what the Bible contains, as well as information about things like cultural background, circumstances, intentions and language of the individual writings. Such study assists in how we understand and interpret the Bible for each new generation. There is reading to bring about action — to motivate us in how we live. Then there is reading which engenders prayer. This type of reading may lead back to reading for knowledge or it may challenge me into some action in my relationship with others, but its primary focus is on prayer.

I find it better to use passages of scripture with which I have considerable familiarity for *lectio*. This helps me avoid speculative journeys which are more to do with satisfying curiosity than with creating a climate for prayer. The Psalms and the Gospels are most commonly the sources I use, or it may be a passage which has gripped me and led me into prayer from the reading of scripture in the daily common prayer of the church. I take the scripture into the silence and stillness of the centre, and listen as I read.

I need to come to *lectio* careful about my intention. So that I make a deliberate affirmation which avoids curiosity and speculation, I often verbalise my desire for encounter with the God who draws me in love. As I read, there may be a word, a phrase or a sentence which speaks to me in a new way. Sometimes the words will act like a healing balm which gives assurance and affirmation as the presence of God is savoured. Sometimes one will experience the truth of this passage:

> The word of God is living and active, sharper than any two-edged sword, piercing until it divides soul from spirit, joints from marrow; it is able to judge the thoughts and intentions of the heart.[1]

Always in love, God may use the scripture to uncover an aspect of living where behaviour or attitudes need to change, reparation made or new directions embraced. It is when the word or phrase leads me into dialogue that *lectio* ceases and *meditatio* begins.

Meditating on the scriptures (*meditatio*)

Meditatio is not the same as meditation if we understand it to mean the activity of thinking and if that thinking about God or some aspect of the spiritual journey. It is not a search for meaning as that can be speculative and therefore inappropriate.

Some of the old masters write that *meditatio* is done with the mouth rather than with the mind. In the Psalms, the Hebrew word we translate as 'meditate' has the root meaning of 'muttering', so we find phrases about meditating with the mouth or the lips. The word or passage is recited — repeated not just in the mind, but with the mouth — so that we are speaking it to ourselves.

So, when it is applicable, I will speak the phrase for *meditatio* slowly and quietly, thus enabling greater participation — involving more of me in the process. The phrase should be assimilated — it should sink into our beings and become part of us — so that it forms us and calls us into prayer.

I recall an old Irish monk from Tarrawarra Abbey in the Yarra Valley talking about the Bible and prayer. He likened the relationship to the cows he milked. The cow, having filled her stomach with the abundant grass, settles down quietly and begins ruminating — regurgitating and digesting what it has eaten — until it is transformed into rich creamy milk.

So the words of scripture are savoured until we become saturated with them and they lead us into *oratio* — further communion with God.

Responding to the scriptures in prayer (*oratio*)

Oratio is the natural outcome of *meditatio*. It is that response of the heart to the word addressed to the God who calls us into loving relationship. If distractions lead us away from this, we should return to the phrase being used for *meditatio*. God leads in this prayer, lovingly prompting our responses. The ensuing dialogue at the centre primarily involves developing friendship with God. It is that which concerns lovers, so there may be things of profound intimacy expressed.

Because it flows from the life of the Trinity — a relationship grounded in mutuality, equality and interdependence — there is an invitation for us to share in the fullness of that reality, in unconditional love and acceptance. Due to the diversity in unity at the centre of the being of God, that all-embracing love entices us, affirming and healing as well as challenging and redirecting.

I referred in a past letter to the claim of C.S. Lewis that our idea of God is not always a divine idea and has to be shattered from time to time. It is in the experience of *oratio* that this often occurs. In the Gospel of Luke, the writer records two of the disciples of Jesus suggesting that they command fire to come down from heaven and consume some unwelcoming people in a Samaritan village, a course of action Jesus rebuked them for.[2] The disciples obviously saw themselves on the side of a divinity which, like a despotic overlord, dispensed vengeance upon the unfortunate ones who had kindled divine wrath.

One of my students shared with me a profound experience of prayerful reflection on this passage from Luke. Out of the experience of *oratio*, she was confronted with being overcome by the thought that God would send the equivalent of a consuming fire from heaven upon another. As well as dealing with her anger over this, more overwhelmingly, she came to the understanding that God was not prepared to own an image more attributable to a popular caricature of a wrathful Zeus. She had long been part of a church which saw itself on the side of a divinity which confronted society with perennial denunciation, disapproval and threats of punishment if it did not conform to what was demanded by divine imperative. This created an idol which needed to be shattered.

It took her a long time to relate to a God who longed for her friendship rather than her service; who sought in and through her to create life-sustaining, liberating, transforming and creative relationships with others. However, through sometimes painful, but always loving encounters with the God of truth at the centre, her understanding and knowledge of God was transfigured. With that also developed her understanding and knowledge of herself.

As she persevered in prayer, she outgrew unhelpful notions of God and began to experience the reality of the love of God — deeper, higher, wider and more powerful than she had ever dared to believe was possible. *Oratio*, therefore, is always a positive and transforming encounter with love and will always be known to be authentic by the fruit it produces.

This is the milieu which is experienced in that prayer which flows out of *lectio* and *meditatio*.

Resting in the scriptures in contemplation (*contemplatio*)

Sometimes what can be a time of intensity and even struggle will lead to complete stillness and rest where no verbal communication is appropriate or necessary. This is termed *contemplatio*. We began in the silence and, having communed with and been embraced by God, we return to the silence.

Most of those who who teach out of this tradition claim that *contemplatio* is not common and that it is essentially a gift — a kind of praying which God may elect to orchestrate.

I do not agree that this kind of prayer is rare. However, it cannot be earned, manipulated or experienced by following a given technique. It is not to be considered superior or encountered only by those with advanced abilities in the spiritual life. It is an expression of intimacy between lovers which may flow out of the experience of *oratio*. It goes past words or images, past sounds and other aspects of the senses. It is communication which is more to do with knowing and being.

I liken it to that which happens between two people who profoundly love one another, who are able to walk together hand in hand for a great distance and realise a level of communication and knowing of each other which has been without words.

Putting the Benedictine pattern into practice

Let me try to share something of the Benedictine pattern which was part of a recent Wednesday night activity. Earlier at Evening Prayer, one of the psalms began with the verse: 'The Lord is my light and my salvation; whom then shall I fear.'[3]

After the scripture readings, the Canticle *The Hymn of the Word* from the Gospel of John was appointed. This contained the words: 'In him was life: and the life was the light of all people. The light shines in the darkness: and the darkness has not overcome it.'[4]

It was dark and the only light in my oratory came from a small oil lamp. I noted the way the tiny flame pushed back the darkness, and began to repeat over and over again these phrases which I had read earlier. As I continued, the key words became the focus, so I repeated them — 'light', 'salvation', 'no fear', 'no darkness' — not so much reflecting upon their meaning, for I was well aware of the significance of the words, but savouring them, allowing them to become part of me and nourish my being. Now this encounter was quite intimate and more in the realm of intuition and feeling than detached and objective analyses. Consequently, I feel somewhat exposed and find writing about it not particularly easy.

However, in the process of gentle dialogue which flowed out after a while, I became aware of an inner 'counsel' advising me not to engage my own darkness, for the life-giving presence of the Light shining in all people has overcome it, transfigured it, brought wholeness of being — and I need not be afraid.

Later as I went to bed, I recalled one of the chants from Taizé and used it as a kind of *mantra* until I lapsed into a deep and refreshing sleep:

Jesus, your light is shining within us.
Let not my doubt or my darkness speak to me.
Jesus, your light is shining within us.
May my heart always welcome your love.

Varying the Benedictine pattern

This is not the only approach to the prayerful reading of scripture. Another approach takes *meditatio* and *oratio* further and specifically encourages the use and development of active imagination.

Some spiritual masters immersed in a way of prayer which does not encourage imaging are very wary of using this faculty. There are many, however, who have found this approach most helpful in the development of their experience of prayer.

The fourteenth-century Carthusian spiritual writer Ludolph of Saxony, in the preface to his *Life of Christ*, exemplifies something of the method of active imagining:

> Read of what has been done [in the Gospel] as though it were happening now... Offer yourself as present to what was said and done through Our Lord Jesus Christ with the whole affective power of your mind... Hear and see these things being narrated as though you were hearing with your own ears and seeing with your own eyes.[5]

This work greatly influenced Ignatius Loyola, the founder of the Jesuits, who developed and championed a similar method of imaginative contemplation and encounter with Jesus in his *Spiritual Exercises*. Others have developed variations based on this method.

One of the members of my community shared with me a somewhat graphic experience of this kind of active imagining. He was using for his meditation the story in the Gospel of John of the encounter between Jesus and a woman at Jacob's Well in the Samaritan city of Sychar.[6] In his imagining, he had seated himself on the side of the well and began a dialogue with Jesus. They began talking about the importance of the well and the need for him to be nourished by the divine life which was being somewhat neglected by him. At that point, Jesus pushed him into the well.

His 'soul friend', being well acquainted with the insights of Carl Jung, was able to understand the link between active imagination and the unconscious. The well was a 'symbol' of the 'centre' where the

Cosmic Lover was longing for an intimate encounter. 'Jesus' here was pushing him into taking notice of what the unconscious was communicating about his inner journey.

I have found methods like this neither personally helpful nor suited to my temperament. Perhaps if I were to persevere, I could benefit from the guidance of someone well practised in the method. So far, I have found the pursuit of active imagining more of a distraction leading away from prayer than a means to embrace it. In the end, I suppose, one has to take up a 'technique' which facilitates a response to the alluring Cosmic Lover.

This further illustrates the maxim that, in the Christian experience, there is no one 'correct' way of prayer. Just as no two lovers express their love in the same way as another two, so no-one responds to the God who calls us into relationship in an identical way to another.

Misusing the Bible

Peter, while I found your comments about the Bible during our last discussion understandable, I was nevertheless saddened that you have encountered its misuse to the extent that you cannot approach it without considerable misgiving.

The Bible has been interpreted and reinterpreted many times over the years, as Christians have used it to bolster all kinds of notions that in the end they have had to abandon as false. As you have pointed out, texts have been used to support arguments such as that the earth is the centre of the universe, that the world was flat, that anaesthetics for women in childbirth were sinful, that slavery was of the divine order, that some races are inferior to others and that women are to be excluded from certain ministries within the Christian community.

History shows that truth and sanity eventually prevail. To quote George Rawson's address to God: 'You have yet more light and truth to break forth from your word.'[7]

God does not seem to allow the church to misuse the Bible for too long without the Spirit guiding it back into truth.[8] This opens up a whole new area of exploration which we must tackle soon. However, it is not the topic of the moment. I'm sorry that you have had to endure people who have tried to use the Bible like a club to beat you into submission to their views. The tragedy is that it has prevented you from experiencing it as a balm to heal and a fire to refine — a living source of dialogue with the God of unconditional love.

I guess that is why I have tried to elaborate at some length about my own journey of prayer with the Bible. In my approach to this great tradition of prayer, I probably leave myself open to the judgment of those who have had a more profound formation in the Benedictine way. It has been crucial for me to adapt it to suit my circumstances, so that my relationship with God could be nourished. Again, a technique or method of prayer can never be an end in itself. If it did not help me to pray, then it would soon have become a rather dull and useless bit of piety which would have rapidly slid into oblivion.

Next Saturday, we picnic and walk in Anakie Gorge. With the abundance of Manna gums along Stony Creek, I'm told that koalas are often to be observed. Never having seen koalas 'in the wild' before, I am hoping they won't be shy. Don't forget that I'm bringing the food.

Alan

5

The prayer that is an invitation to love

Dear Peter,
With the rather heady discussion about what we call 'intercession' yesterday, I was glad there was some relief in rock-hopping along Stony Creek, watching the blue wrens foraging in the scrub and, above all, finding some koalas asleep in the trees around the picnic area.

You are right! As popularly understood, the prayer we call 'intercession' can often seem to be ridiculous. You drew my attention to Terry Lane's penetrating and humorous list of problems with prayer in *God: The Interview*[1] and asked for my opinion. Speaking for God, Lane caricatures certain assumptions which he believes are at the foundation of Christian prayer for others. The first is that God is interested in what some individual human wants.

(He then claims that God is *not* interested!) Second, he states that God is not paying attention and needs to be reminded of what is going on. Third, that if asked nicely, God will do something, but through laziness, vanity, inattention or churlishness, God has chosen not to.

In a biting paragraph, and again speaking for God, he gives an illustration:

> Here is a whole church full of people praying that I will cure the cancer of someone they know. Now, being a good God, if I could have cured her cancer, would I not already have done so? Am I so distracted that I haven't noticed? Am I so vain that I want to see a bit of grovelling before I will stir myself to pass a miracle? What on earth do you people think is going on?[2]

Intercessory prayer does not have its origins in human need or desire. When we began discussing the Christian understanding of prayer, we noted that it is not an activity which begins with us. Essentially, prayer is God's activity. It has its origins and its outcome in God and, when we are praying, it is in response to God. It is being in tune with that which is going on in the being of God.

God is not some heavenly sugar daddy who can be manipulated into granting all kinds of special favours. Nor is God like some cosmic gambling machine, with prayer akin to inserting coins and pressing buttons in the hope that the jackpot will pour into the laps of persistent punters. That these beliefs might seem to be behind the prayer practices of some Christians is rightly to be parodied, but they do not negate the prayer of intercession. They only make mistaken assumptions appear ridiculous.

Involvement in intercessory prayer, like all that we label 'prayer', is a process of learning and discovery. It confronts us with profound mysteries, as we struggle with the collapse of our false ideas of God. As our relationship with God is refined in the experience of prayer, we seek to embrace new truths.

Jesus makes a rather homely claim about a God who is, contrary to Terry Lane's first assumption, not removed from the tapestry of human existence:

> Are not five sparrows sold for two pennies? Yet not one of them is forgotten in God's sight. But even the hairs of your head are all counted. Do not be afraid; you are of more value than many sparrows.[3]

From their experience of life, many Christians would affirm the reality of this saying. No person seriously involved in the life of prayer would claim that God is inattentive or needs to be reminded about anything. Nor would they assert that God had to be pampered, placated or cajoled into a response.

Intercession is an invitation to share in God's activity

Rather than seeing intercession as trying to involve God in some particular matter, the reverse is true — God seeks to involve us. Let me try to explain this hypothetically. My friend Mary has been going through a time of great stress and has become physically ill. If I were using the Terry Lane model, I suppose I would express my concern in telling God all about it as if he needed to be informed. Then, I would ask God in the nicest and most persuasive way I could to remove the stress and heal her. The assumptions about the divinity behind that approach are absurd.

As I have experienced it, intercession works in a totally different way. Let me use the hypothetical story of Mary as an example. God invites me to intercession through the solitude and silence of centring, and I become attuned to the prayer going on in the being of God. It is neither Mary's need which motivates the prayer, nor does it flow from my emotional responses. How I feel about a particular situation may be a complete hindrance to grasping the divine perspective.

God is the source of the prayer. God may evoke profound compassion for Mary and this may embrace verbalising my own concerns for her. I need, however, to watch that my concerns do not get in the way. The essential focus is not Mary and her needs, but God's concerns. I need to respond to the direction of the prayer which I encounter flowing from God.

As I surrender to the prayer, I open myself to the possibility of being a channel of love — of God's creative and healing energies. It is not a matter of telling God what to do about Mary, but the privilege of being drawn into an intimate sharing in God's concern about her. God may chose to leave the matter there. On the other hand, I might be nudged into making contact with her to assist the alleviation of her stress in some practical way, or to the enhancing of the God-given 'natural' regime in which she will move back into wholeness.

Intercession is an invitation to change

Because at the centre we know and experience God as Love, there can be no creative intercessory prayer without unconditional love. The experience of holding some person or situation in the presence of God can often result in being confronted with one's own inability to love. This means that first one must allow God to deal with this before there can be any thought of being a channel for the love of God to others.

Coupled with this is the exposure of other

negative attitudes related to a lack of love. To 'think God's thoughts' in prayer sometimes means being confronted with the inner hindrances of prejudice, intolerance, ignorance and fear. Thus, this encounter will sometimes involve the struggle of interior conversion, with the necessity of aligning one's attitudes and inner disposition with those which belong to God. If one is not completely at one with the movement of the love of God, then the prayer becomes counterproductive and a travesty.

Peter, I think you may be right in your observation that it seems to be the lot of some 'religious' people to be blatantly narrow, superficial and rigid. This leads to a paralysis of spirit that makes them insensitive to the leading of God. Their image of God is distorted and they appear unable to understand how their views could possibly differ from those of the divinity they invoke. Their attempts at prayer are sometimes exercises in self-delusion. They are more often focussed on their own sense of righteousness, so they fail to hear the voice of the God who longs to rechannel all their zeal in the way of love.

The prayer of intercession is serious business. It not only means being in the presence of God for others. It also involves being changed oneself. In prayer, one enters the crucible of love. God as a refiner seeking a pure alloy will apply the heat so that the dross surfaces and is painfully scraped away. Only then can there be any authentic intercession.

The need for change is apparent when with true openness in prayer we look at our heart, our centre. Here we find in microcosm a replica in miniature of the world at large. The great issues which are being faced in international conflicts, civil strife and sectional rivalries have their counterparts within us. There is no point in my yearning for an end to such things as sectarian bitterness in Northern Ireland and expressing that longing in prayer, if I cannot confront the manifestation of that bitterness within me. In my prayer, I am made aware that I have no power to deal with the conflict overseas, but I can respond to the divine invitation to reconcile the issues within myself.

I am intrigued by those who claim a connection between interior struggle and cosmic conflict. I remain an agnostic in this matter, but I still wonder. A few years back, a friend shared something of her interior struggle to deal with the walls she had created within herself which prevented her from growing towards a greater integration and wholeness of being. As she sought to cooperate with the promptings of God at the centre, she experienced an interior metamorphosis as fears and prejudices began to collapse.

While this was going on, she was also aware of

the creative energies of God praying within her concerning the political developments in Eastern Europe. At the very time she knew an inner liberation with the collapse of interior barriers, the news came of the first cracks in the Berlin Wall.

I find this a fascinating coincidence to contemplate! Whatever one makes of such apparent coincidences, I believe there is no doubt that there can be no praying for wholeness in a broken and disordered world if we are not prepared for that work to be accomplished within ourselves.

Intercession is directed to a God who has suffered so much

Behind the practice of intercessory prayer lurks the greatest dilemma of the human journey, the dilemma of suffering and evil. Yesterday, Peter, you raised the possibility of 'reincarnation' as a solution. Perhaps people believe in reincarnation because it lends support to the idea that there is an ultimate justice and that overwhelming evil can be redressed.

I still affirm the Christian belief in one attempt at life. I am aware that probably belief in reincarnation has been held by the majority of humans who have ever lived and to give it a scant mention is not to discount it. For me, however, it produces as many problems as it solves and still leaves me with the same great ethical paradoxes.

There is the paradox of suffering, particularly when experienced by those whom we would term 'innocent' or 'undeserving'. There is the enigma of evil in so many contexts: in the experience of war and oppressive political regimes; in the massive industry which gorges itself on the fearful trade in weapons of mass annihilation; in the rape and pollution of the earth by economic greed; in the devastating perversity of so-called 'natural' disasters which wreak havoc on thousands of people. While there is mystery at the centre of such suffering and evil, we know that most of it is caused or aggravated by the ignorance or deliberate choices of humankind, choices which cause illusion. This illusion produces a paralysis which renders it incapable of responding to the God who in love longs for us.

These paradoxes have exercised greater minds than mine and still not come to any resolution. There is nothing I can say which would add anything to the wisdom we have been able to embrace. However, as I struggle with these things at the centre, listening in the silence, there are a number of images which engage me and cause me to speculate.

One image is of a God with open wounds. The Gospels present us with a Jesus who would not engage the world in terms of its dominating political systems, its destructive greed, its lust for power and control. We are confronted with one who in profound humiliation and alienation is stretched out in crucifixion; one who in resurrection is encountered with wounds, not covered over, closed or scarred. Unlike the 'beast', the image of evil in the Book of Revelation which is represented as having a mortal wound which has been healed,[4] these wounds have not healed. They are taken into the Trinity and continue to perplex us as we contemplate a divine love which is vulnerable and suffers in the midst of creation.

This God is not 'above' us, so that we operate in an illusion that there is an omnipotence which will intervene in our lives. God is within our creatureliness — around it, sustaining it, suffering with and transfiguring it. This is the God I encounter in the silence at the centre. This God gently seeks to engage and court rather than intrude, to co-create with those who will respond. It is to this God, who has suffered so much, that I intercede on behalf of those who suffer and face evil.

You may recall in the *The Magician's Nephew*, one of the Narnia Chronicles of C.S. Lewis, Digory comes to Aslan the Lion asking for some magical fruit to heal his sick mother. Aslan does not answer. Nor does he seem to care about Digory's concern or the illness of his mother. At a second encounter with Aslan, in tears as hope fades for his mother, he is surprised by Aslan's reaction:

Up till then he had been looking at the Lion's great front feet and the huge claws on them; now, in his despair, he looked up at its face. What he saw surprised him as much as anything in his whole life. For the tawny face was bent down near his own and (wonder of wonders) great shining tears stood in the Lion's eyes. They were such big, bright tears compared with Digory's own that, for a moment, he felt as if the Lion must really be sorrier about his Mother than he was himself.[5]

Digory discovers that the 'shining tears' in the eyes Aslan are an assurance of the Lion's great love which shares his suffering. This is an allegory about the Cosmic Lover who embraces the suffering of the whole human race. Christians see this enigma in the suffering of the crucified Jesus who continues to take into himself the pain of creation.

Intercession is an invitation to engage in subversion

The prayer of intercession not only involves confrontation with the pain of the world as it connects with our own interior journey; it must lead to our commitment to the transformation of the world. If our prayer is authentic, we will not be able to avoid involvement in the actualisation of that petition in the Lord's Prayer: 'Your Kingdom come'.

Nikos Kazantzakis, in his autobiography *Report to Greco*, writes of a visit to a Cretan monastery as part of his spiritual searching:

It was the wise Father Joachim who, clapping his hands as though I was a pullet, shooed me away. 'Return to the world,' he cried. 'In this day and age the world is the true monastery; that is where you will become a saint.'[6]

The controversial American priest and political activist, Daniel Berrigan, goes even further by describing the pursuit of prayer as 'a subversive activity... a political act of the highest value, implying the riskiest consequences of those taking part'.[7]

Peter, I cringe when you point out to me the contradictions in so much of what has purported to be Christianity. Sadly, human history is riddled with grotesque examples of zealous religious people who have sought to establish their particular views of the meaning of 'Your kingdom come'. The means they have employed often have surpassed the excesses of the worst totalitarian regimes which have scarred humanity in recent years. They have sought to take the cross, turn it upside down and, sharpening one end, turn it into a sword.

Brute force, violence and political manipulation are all foreign to the teaching of Jesus and it is a travesty that there have been those who claim to be disciples who have exercised power in a way he would not own. The commonwealth of God does not come by exercising power as we have commonly come to experience such things. It will come as we engage in non-violent peacemaking, suffering in love alongside those who are victims of injustice and prejudice, and seeking to care for those who are sick and needy discarded by society.

Jesus spoke of our seeing and serving him in the needy and marginalised people around us:

> Then the king will say. . . I was hungry and you have me food, I was thirsty and you gave me something to drink, I was a stranger and you welcomed me, I was naked and you gave me clothing, I was sick and you took care of me, I was in prison and you visited me.
>
> Then the righteous will answer him, 'Lord, when was it that we saw you hungry and gave you food, or thirsty and gave you something to drink? And when was it that we saw you a stranger and welcomed you, or naked and gave you clothing? And when was it that we saw you sick or in prison and visited you?'
>
> And the king will answer them, 'Truly I tell you, just as you did it to one of the least of these who are members of my family, you did it to me.'[8]

The God of unconditional love, whom Christians see in the life of Jesus, does not draw us into prayer that makes us so heavenly minded that we are of no earthly use. While we experience God at the centre in intimate personal relationship, we will also be confronted with the realisation that God is also encountered in the fabric and structures of human society. Taking up the image from the Hebrew scriptures of God encountered in the burning bush by Moses,[9] Christian writer Joan Puls aptly entitled her recent publication about finding God in every human situation, *Every Bush is Burning*.[10] I find this a fascinating image to take into my prayer. If prayer does not have a clear human and social focus, it cannot claim to be Christian prayer.

You asked whether prayer changes a situation. I don't believe that prayer in itself changes anything. As I said in my first letter, prayer is God's activity in us. God initiates prayer. In response to God, I am drawn into that relationship which we call 'prayer'. If things or people are changed, it is God who does it.

Well, Peter, I hope that I have addressed some of the issues which your raised during yesterday's walk. If you can be patient with me, I will leave further reflection on the other matters to a subsequent letter. James and Tricia have asked me to be the celebrant of their marriage at the end of next month in the University Chapel. I am very happy about that! David and Jane have offered their home for the small reception they were planning and to undertake the catering as well, so it looks like being quite an event. I hope all is well with you.

With warmest regards,

Alan

6

Shared encounter of prayer in the Christian community

Dear Peter,
The presence of Jahn and Magda at lunch at the 'Windmill' yesterday certainly brought some issues into sharp relief! I was heartened by the way Bruno seemed to arrive at the right moment with plates of wonderful Italian food. It helped to keep the proceedings convivial and assisted greatly in oiling the machinery of respectful dialogue.

I knew that we would eventually have to deal with matters concerning the institutional face of Christianity. It is not possible to talk about the spiritual journey and the life of prayer from a Christian perspective without dealing with the relationship of the individual and the church. I was glad to be able to add my own 'horror stories' of incompetence and little-minded power groups.

I have to confess that I was a little stunned when Magda so vehemently took me to task for still being 'in the church' and, therefore in her mind, tacitly supporting its dark side.

Unlike Magda, I have also seen the Christian community at its best, with noble and beautiful people who convincingly image the reality and attractiveness of Jesus. I am not able to condemn it, as she does, with so much anger. However, I doubt that I will ever forget her diagnosis of the church as 'a malignant cancer in the body of society which needs immediate radical surgery'.

I have been greatly saddened by the stories Magda related about the insensitive condemnation and rejection she and her friends have experienced at the hands of people claiming to be Christians. Yesterday, however, I thought that at the end of our long lunch she might have become a little less convinced about her view that there is nothing of value in the Christian tradition.

So far, in our discussion about the Christian experience of the life of prayer, we have focussed upon the individual's relationship with God, for that is ultimately how we experience it. But it is not the whole story.

So again, at your suggestion, I will put on paper a few of my thoughts.

The value of the shared prayers
of the Christian community

When, in response to the Cosmic Lover, we enter
into the silence of prayer at the centre, we are often
conscious of an aloneness in the presence of God.
As I said in an earlier letter, while the experience of
prayer is intimate and personal, it is never private.
The adventure of communion with God is never in
isolation, for we are drawn into community.

In the Christian experience of these things, being
drawn into relationship with God also involves
being drawn into relationship with others who are
fellow travellers on the spiritual journey. The fellow travellers comprise the church. This is no mere
human construct. It is the creation of God and is a
reflection of the life of the Trinity as God creatively
reaches out welcoming all things into a vital relationship. I experience my adventure with God as a
member of the church.

I can understand Magda and those who have
found the church as 'organised religion' disappoint-
ing and somewhat trivial. Yet I have also
experienced the church at its best and you'll not be
surprised at my claim that I do not think I could
survive for very long without it.

I don't want to push the difference between the
church as human institution and the church as a

living, spiritual dynamic too much. As I have said, the former can be frustrating and seemingly irrelevant. In the latter, I see strength and beauty and in that I am totally 'at home'. Let me explain a little of how this relates to my experience of the spiritual journey.

The apostle Paul uses an intriguing image to describe the church. In writing to the Christians at Corinth, he claims that in baptism we become part of Christ. Collectively, he calls Christians 'the body of Christ' and 'individually members of it'.[1] By implication, then, there is a strong 'organic' link between the individual and Christ, as well as between each Christian. Being 'church' is essentially a matter of relationship.

From the beginning, Christians encountered God *together*. They prayed *together*. In the Acts of the Apostles, it is stated:

> They devoted themselves to the apostles' teaching and fellowship, to the breaking of bread and the prayers. . . day by day, attending the temple together and breaking bread in their homes.[2]

Rather than the sum total of individual and personal encounters with God constituting their collective experience, it was the involvement in prayer together which sustained their personal prayer.

Prayer at the transition of day and night, at dawn and at dusk, was part of the Christian experience from the beginning. Daily prayer together encompassed the singing of psalms, the reading of the scriptures as well as prayers. In the Christian community to which I belong, there is a tradition of communal morning and evening prayer which has its origins in the practice of the first Christians. This has long been an essential part of my journey with God. A list of psalms and readings for each day, called a 'lectionary', enables an orderly recitation of the psalter and reading through the Bible.

Sometimes my circumstances have prevented me from being able to pray with others. Yet, even while praying the psalms and reading the scriptures apart from others, I am never alone. I experience an almost tangible solidarity with those who, in so many other places, are involved in the same common prayer.

As I mentioned in an earlier letter, it is most often out of the psalms or the Bible readings from the common prayer of the church that I find material for the Benedictine practice of prayer. My personal prayer is sustained by the experience of common prayer.

The objective nature of common prayer helps to prevent me from being overwhelmed by the subjective experiences of my life. I may be tired or unwell, in the middle of some personal crisis or conflict, or just plain lazy or bored. I may be struggling with some issues with God which make personal prayer more difficult.

Particularly when I am with others, the daily common prayer carries me. I am present — perhaps only with my body as my mind may be distracted — and that in itself signifies my desire to respond to God, the Cosmic Lover.

I found this particularly so during that period a couple of years ago when I was being treated for lymphoma with chemotherapy. You will remember that I was often completely exhausted and it was a struggle to muster the energy to focus on anything other than how I was feeling. At these times, I found the immense value of the non-cerebral mantric forms of prayer, the simple chants from Taizé and the tactile comfort of a prayer cord from the Russian Christians.

Above all, I was thankful that the common prayer of the church went on, reflecting the cosmic prayer at the heart of the universe of which we have spoken. Others often came and prayed with me the morning and evening psalms and read the scriptures, and this sustained me until I was able more fully to take up again the adventure of personal prayer at the centre.

The value of the shared Psalter in moulding prayer

Yesterday, you expressed some bewilderment that the Psalter — the hymns and poetry of the Hebrew people some of which have been around for nearly three millennia — could be used in the prayer of an Australian Christian at the end of the twentieth century. I guess the fact that they have been around for so long, and as such used by millions to give substance to the entire span and depth of human feelings and aspirations, must speak for itself.

I have lived with the psalms for over thirty years. They have been part of the daily common prayer I have shared with others in many different places and circumstances — recited with brother monks in a chapel created out of a stone cowshed in the south-west of England; sung in choir in an Australian cathedral; prayed alone in a small cave in a desolate gorge on the Western Australian coast. Yet in these and many other places, the words of the psalms have given shape to my prayer: in times of joy and thanksgiving; in times of sadness and personal grief; on occasions of profound adoration and worship; and, conversely, in feelings of abandonment and the need to express anger.

My experiences when written could become encyclopaedic! I will not try to deal with them all, but

let me illustrate with a few. As I do so, I shall
attempt to show how I see them as a shared experience. Some Psalms have a very personal application
for me, but I am conscious that I share with others
as they read these words their own personal appli-
cations.

The first example is a extract from Psalm 104:

> How many are your works, O Lord!
> In wisdom you have made them all.
> The earth is full of your riches.
> There is the wide sea, vast and wide,
> with its moving swarms past counting,
> living things great and small.
> The ships are moving there
> and the monsters you made to play with.

I know you delight in branding me naïve when I
speak of God delighting in creation, but I will per-
sist. I truly believe that the cosmos is born out of
the love and joy experienced in the Trinity.

One of the pleasures of living for a few years on
the west coast of Australia was the opportunity to
observe and encounter dolphins and whales. I never
cease to be amazed at the intelligence and sense of
humour of the dolphins and the grace and beauty of
huge whales. The Psalm gives me a profound understanding of God who 'plays with the huge sea
creatures'. It also reminds me of the dependence of

the creation upon the Creator, as the psalm goes on
to say:

> All of these look to you
> to give them their food in due season.
> You give it, they gather it up:
> you open your hand, they have their fill.
> You hide your face, they are dismayed;
> you take back your spirit, they die,
> returning to the dust from which they came.
> You send forth your spirit, they are created
> and you renew the face of the earth.[3]

Sometimes, there is a longing for God as I wait at
the centre, trying to respond to the desire created
within me by the Cosmic Lover. The poet who
composed Psalm 63 seems to have had a similar
experience when he sings:

> O God, you are my God, for you I long;
> for you my soul is thirsting.
> My body pines for you
> like a dry, weary land without water.[4]

Another way the Psalms mould my praying is in
the 'permission' they give to express a lot of my
negative feelings. Once when I was let down by
someone I considered to be a close friend, I went
through weeks of feeling betrayed. Lies were told
and my integrity was brought into question. For

some time I found it difficult to deal with the anger generated. Psalm 55 gave me words which helped me verbalise in the presence of God the hurt I was experiencing:

> If this has been done by an enemy
> I could bear his taunts.
> If a rival had risen against me,
> I could hide from him.
> But it is you, my own companion,
> my intimate friend!
> (How close was the friendship between us.)
> We walked together in harmony
> in the house of God. . .
> As for me, I will cry to God
> and the Lord will save me.
> Evening, morning and at noon
> I will cry and lament. . .
> His speech is softer than butter,
> but war is in his heart.
> His words are smoother than oil,
> but they are naked swords.[5]

There were times when I could put my own feelings into the imprecatory verses. These alarm many Christians as they appear to be inappropriate responses in the face of injustice. The teaching of Jesus about loving and forgiving one's enemy and turning the other cheek have sometimes been for me a counsel of perfection or, more so, a counsel of despair. Until I was able to take on board the teaching of Jesus, I needed to express to God the rage within me. So, despite the contradictions, there was nowhere else to direct the anger but on to God!

> May death fall suddenly upon them!
> Let them go to the grave:
> for wickedness dwells in their homes
> and deep in their hearts.[6]

One of my mentors encouraged me to use these 'prayers of aggression' as he termed them. Only in God can the destructive hurts and angers be dissipated which are caused by dysfunctional human relationships and the adverse experiences of life. In this way, the aggression can be dealt with and that which might spill out into further destructive conflict can be healed. It is in this light that I can understand the Psalm which demonstrates the the need of a people taken into captivity in a foreign country to express their rage at the injustice done to them. Their land had been invaded and their children slaughtered; 'by the rivers of Babylon' they sat and wept:

> O daughter of Babylon you that lay waste:
> happy shall he be who serves you as you have served us;
> Happy shall he be who takes *your* little ones:
> and dashes them against the stones.[7]

When I was confronted with the diagnosis of a life-threatening illness and there was no-one around with whom I could talk, I experienced a few days of acute depression. Unable to escape a sense of being abandoned by God as well as everyone else, I recall sitting on the end of a pier in tears with my Psalter opened at Psalm 88:

> Friend and neighbour you have taken away:
> my one companion is darkness.[8]

Fortunately this did not last for long, but the Psalm gave me a means of putting my confusion and disoriented feelings into some objective expression and a framework in which I could take these into my prayer.

Sometimes, the Psalter enables there to be a more obviously shared vision. While I was a conscript in the Australian Army at the time of the Vietnam War, I had two close Christian friends with whom I had shared the somewhat gruelling three months of initial recruit training. A few months later, they were in the thick of the Vietnam conflict just as the Tet offensive commenced. The news coming back via the newspapers and their own letters indicated that life for them was hardly a picnic. They were constantly in danger of being killed. Comrades were dying or suffering major injuries.

I could only try to imagine what they were experiencing as I lay each evening in relative safety on my bunk in the barracks of the Second Field Ambulance at Puckapunyal. As I used the night prayer service of Compline each evening, it was Psalm 91 which I was able to pray in solidarity with Dan and Neale and the many others in that part of the world not known to me personally:

> You who live in the shelter of the Most High. . .
> will say to the Lord, 'My refuge and my fortress;
> my God in whom I trust.'
> For he will deliver you from the snare of the fowler
> and from the deadly pestilence. . .
> You will not fear the terror of the night,
> or the arrow that flies by day,
> or the pestilence that stalks in the darkness,
> or the destruction that wastes at noonday.
> A thousand may fall at your side,
> ten thousand at your right hand,
> but it will not come near you. . .
> No evil shall befall you,
> no scourge come near your tent. . .[8]

In due course, I was glad to welcome them back home, at least physically unscathed at the end of the tour of service, and thankful to God that the words of the Psalm had helped me pray and cope with the special anxieties of the time.

I am also helped when the Psalms can reflect the prayer of the whole Christian community or the cry of humanity in the midst of its needs. I may not be able personally to identify with what is being expressed, yet I am only too aware that, despite the liberation of many in recent days from oppressive regimes, there are still people being persecuted for their religious or political beliefs. There are still those who because of race or nationality, or some other factor which causes the powerful to push them to the margins, are made to suffer greatly.

The cries for justice and liberation found in the Psalms can become their cries and, as part of the Body of Christ, I can pray with them. Taking up that fascinating image again, the apostle Paul can write:

> If one member suffers, all suffer together with it;
> if one member is honoured, all rejoice together with it.[9]

In this light, when other human beings are suffering, the Psalms give scope for others to cry out in pain with and for them. I find then that while I may not have specific personal application for the words of the Psalms being prayed by the church on a particular day, they are the prayer of others in the Body of Christ and I can pray in solidarity with and for them.

Yesterday, Magda said she was not aware of anything in the Christian spiritual tradition like that of the guru. There were no Christian spiritual masters who gave assistance to those who were searching for guidance on the spiritual journey. How wrong can one become!

I think I have written enough in today's letter, so tomorrow I will take up the relationship between the individual journey and the collective experience of the Christian community in some consideration of the Christian spiritual guides.

With warmest regards as always,

Alan

7

Ministry of spiritual guides in the prayer journey

Dear Peter,

I promised another letter in which I would take some of Magda's issues a bit further. On Thursday at the 'Windmill', she asked where the Christian gurus or spiritual guides were. I suppose that having explored some of the religions of the East in their 'grand tour' at the beginning of the seventies, she and Jahn have become more aware of the tradition of the guru in Hinduism or the spiritual masters of Zen than they are of any similar tradition among Christians.

On the surface, at least in some of the Christian communities of the West, Magda's observations seem to have some substance. I think there are some special factors which have contributed to this.

Magda and Jahn have really only experienced a

fairly narrow Christianity. After the controversies in the Christianity of sixteenth-century Europe, with the children of the Reformation championing individual direct access to God through Christ the one mediator, there was not perceived to be a great need for the ministry of special spiritual guides. There were certainly women and men in this tradition who exercised unique ministries of guidance in the life of prayer, but not in the manner of personal spiritual direction experienced in other traditions.

Consequently, because it was at best not seen to be vital, and at worst under the suspicion of fostering priestcraft, this ministry has not significantly flourished among them. There has been misunderstanding — even antagonism — to the mystical aspects of prayer as something which might debilitate 'practical Christianity'. There has been a fear of being 'so heavenly minded that they are of no earthly use'. To major in the pursuit of the life of prayer and specially to look for another to be a director or guide has been thought a luxury which, given the state of the world, cannot be afforded.

Jahn has had most to do with Christians who have largely thought like this. When he began to seek for someone among them to assist him in his spiritual search, he did not, sadly, meet with a satisfying response and, on that somewhat superficial encounter, dismissed Christianity as being 'empty'.

While his criticism is not without foundation, it is unfair to the Reformation tradition in the West and to Christianity as a whole.

In the context of our conversation with Jahn and Magda, you asked whether having a spiritual guide was a necessary part of the Christian experience of the life of prayer. At the outset I would say 'No'. If, as we have claimed earlier, the Cosmic Lover at the centre of the universe is the prime mover in the relationship which is prayer; if prayer is essentially not our undertaking but God's activity in us; if it is God who sets the agenda and directs the flow of prayer; then the intrusion of a so-called 'guide' would seem superfluous.

I think I have mentioned to you the counsel of one of my mentors: 'The only way to learn about prayer is to pray.' Of course, he was correct. Much of my own learning in the way of prayer has been by the seat of my pants.

Yet, while this is true, there have been those — dare I say — sent by God, who have been wonderful 'midwives'.[1] They have assisted in the painful and somewhat messy business of bringing to birth new developments in my relationship with God. I have begun to see that while God is certainly the prime mover in the spiritual journey, God also uses others in the Christian community to facilitate that relationship.

While there may be a dearth of spiritual guides

in some parts of the church today, there is a long and rich tradition of those who in their day were great guides for others in the spiritual pilgrimage, many of whom wrote of their insights and experience so that other generations might be assisted as well.

In this letter, Peter, my little excursion into history will of necessity be superficial and selective, but it is an endeavour to serve my point. The Christian spiritual tradition has certainly not been without its spiritual guides.

Spiritual guides in the early church

The first major flowering of spiritual guides appeared among those we now call the *abbas* and *ammas* (spiritual fathers and mothers) of the desert. This took place largely in the wilderness of Egypt. There were those who thought that the legalisation of Christianity by the Emperor Constantine early in the fourth century meant a reconciliation between the church and the state which was too facile.

You may recall that in a past letter, when issues concerning intercession were raised, I referred to 'the centre' being a microcosm — a replica in miniature — of the world at large. There were those who fled from the cities, which were now 'Christian', into the deserts and wilderness areas in order to do battle in prayer in the human heart. Some lived alone in caves or small huts, while others formed themselves into loose communities.

Those of us living at the end of the second millennium could be forgiven for finding this movement alien and somewhat strange. However, in its day it was a movement of considerable spiritual significance which produced a great flourishing of wise and discerning men and women who were greatly sought after for guidance. Christians would travel great distances into the wilderness seeking help in the spiritual journey and the way of prayer from an *amma* or *abba*. They were not mere dispensers of advice or teachers of a particular technique. They reflected the life-engendering and nurturing role of a father or mother, seeking to develop the inner life of the person who had come, through prayer, discernment and pastoral care.

Some idea of their counsel is available for us today in a collection of anecdotes and opinions known as the *Apophthegmata Patrum: The Sayings of the Fathers.*[2]

This tradition was carried into Western Christianity by John Cassian who, with his friend Germanus, had spend several years learning from the great spiritual guides of Egypt. Cassian, through his *Institutes* and *Conferences*, had considerable influence on the Benedictines who were responsible for the evangelisation of so much of western Europe. Admittedly, this spiritual guide movement was largely confined to the monastic movement, but in this context, the ministry of the 'holy man' and 'holy woman' who could guide in the life of prayer became a part of the Christian experience even if it did not flourish in the same way as it did in the East.

At its best, the monastic movement provided this ministry, not only for those who chose to live within its bounds as nuns and monks, but also to the whole Christian community. Thus the American writer on spirituality, Richard Foster, can claim: 'In the Middle Ages, not even the greatest saints attempted the depths of the inward journey without the help of a spiritual director.'[3]

In other Christian cultures, the ministry of the spiritual guide has been greatly valued and flourished. Among the Celtic Christians, there was the *anmchara* (an Irish term for a spiritual guide). This ministry may have been one already valued in pre-Christian times and subsequently 'baptised'. Nevertheless, Celtic Christians held the ministry of the soul friend as essential.

Hence the proverb attributed by some to St Brigit: 'Anyone without a soul friend (*anmchara*) is like a body without a head.' The *anmchara* was not necessarily a ministry of the ordained — more often, a laywoman or layman specially gifted was sought out for this ministry.

Spiritual guides amongst Eastern Christians

Christians in the Eastern Orthodox tradition have always highly valued the ministry of the spiritual guide. I remember your comment as we drove to the Brisbane Ranges recently that there were at least seven domed churches in a small area on the edge of town — even some with gilded onion-shaped domes. These belong to the people who have migrated here in recent times — the Serbs, the Russians, the Ukrainians, the Macedonians, the Copts, the Syrians, the Greeks.

In this country, we have been greatly enriched by people from parts of the world where Orthodoxy has been the major religion. Some have suffered for their faith under oppressive political regimes. They are saturated in the tradition of holy women and men who have been a bright lamp in helping others to pray. Other Christians can only be enriched by what they may be able to share with us.

The Sydney Orthodox theologian John Chryssavgis has helped me understand the ministry of the spiritual guide in his tradition by speaking of 'two levels' on which, in his experience, the Christian community exists and functions: the hierarchical and the spiritual, the outward and the inner, the institutional and the charismatic:

In this sense, the *geron* (spiritual father) exists alongside the apostles. Although not ordained through the episcopal laying-on of hands, the spiritual father is essentially a prophetic person who has received his *charisma* directly from the Spirit of God.[4]

Now I'm sorry that this all may be getting a bit technical, but in order to show the defects in the criticisms of Magda and Jahn, I want to underline that particularly among Eastern Christians there has never been a dearth of spiritual guides — in fact they are seen to be as vital and necessary a part of the Christian community as the bishops and other 'institutional' leaders.

You will be aware of Staretz Zossima from your reading of Dostoevsky. Russian Christians have experienced at different times a special blossoming in the ministry of the *staretz* — the 'old man' or the specially gifted spiritual guide. Many Russian Christians, particularly before the Revolution, were assisted by these God-given guides who facilitated and encouraged growth in the life of prayer.

Spiritual guides amongst Western Christians

Now there will be those who will take issue with me over this view, but I believe that for some time in the West, the ministry of the spiritual guide has been hampered by a strong link with sacramental confession. This gave the ministry of direction a strongly priestly element and made the major focus the negative things which had happened in the past. Thus, it became a ministry of correcting faults, dealing with matters of conscience or granting absolution.

While there may be a need in the ministry of the spiritual guide to encourage the confession of things that are wrong so that there is freedom to grow in the inner life, it is not the main purpose of this ministry. The link with sacramental confession strongly hampered the development of the ministries of laywomen and laymen which were not so hindered in the East. Along with this, much of this ministry focussed on the monasteries, which also tended to create a climate in which the ministry and practice of spiritual friendship was not seen to be a vital part of 'secular' Christianity.

Many write as if the ministry of the spiritual guide is for a kind of spiritual elite. The Jesuit James Walsh, for example, claims that the ministry of the spiritual director is only necessary when one becomes aware of 'God's *special* call to perfection'.[5] This perpetuates a view that growth in a mature relationship with the Cosmic Lover is not for the 'ordinary' Christian. As a consequence, there has been an impoverishment for so many of a vital life of prayer.

Of course, I acknowledge that the West has produced many great spiritual teachers like Ignatius

Loyola, Teresa, John of the Cross, Francis de Sales and de Caussade — to mention but a few — but my feelings about the practice of spiritual direction in the West is that it has been seriously hampered. So the English writer Michael Hollings can note:

> There are fewer people who manage to live a life of prayer. Fewer people still live out a life of prayer and then write about it. I think of a string of names from the past. But where do we go today? Not so long ago, a Buddhist student at Birmingham University asked me: 'Where today can I find someone who is teaching the kind of prayer I read about in *The Cloud of Unknowing*'[6]

My own Christian community has not been without its holy men and women who have been greatly valued spiritual guides and we have the writings of some of them to continue to engender inspiration. It has, however, not escaped major decrement from the same attitudes which pervade the rest of the Western experience.

Nevertheless, I believe we are living in a fascinating time! In this country at least, there has been a growing demand from 'ordinary' Christians for 'soul friends' who will help them as they seek to respond to the God who calls them into relationship 'at the centre'. Some have been thrown in the deep end by the requests which have come to them.

I have spoken to many who have had this thrust

upon them. Some are among the ordained, but many are women and men who could hardly be dubbed 'pseudo-clergy'.

John Chryssavgis notes that often it is the spiritual daughters and sons who 'give birth' to spiritual mothers and fathers. Recognising in them a maturity in the life of prayer born out of considerable spiritual struggle in encounter with the Cosmic Lover, the ministry of spiritual guide is called forth. It is the seeker for a guide who reveals that person as one 'pregnant with God'.[7]

In many parts of this country, there are now people and places in all Christian traditions which seek to recognise, encourage and facilitate spiritual guides who will act as 'midwives' in the life of prayer. It is not easy to assess whether this is the beginning of a new manifestation of this ministry. Only time will tell! But I find the signs most encouraging.

In Melbourne, there is a sizable group of women and men, lay people as well as ordained, who have had this ministry placed on their shoulders and who meet regularly for prayer and mutual support as they seek to respond to what God is doing in and through them. There has also developed a network of spiritual guides around Australia who are in regular contact and meet annually in conference to assist one another in the growth of their ministry.

I have had a number of significant spiritual guides throughout my journey in the life of prayer. Initially, I was greatly helped by a wise and prayerful priest, who had a substantial experience of the mystical tradition.

He introduced me to the writings of such spiritual giants as Julian of Norwich, Ramon Lull and Richard Rolle, as well as Puritans like Samuel Rutherford.

He introduced me to the writing of Amy Carmichael, a woman of great courage and mystical spirituality, and helped me obtain many of her books and a little of her unpublished work. Because of its vibrant 'catholicity', it has been a constant source of encouragement and inspiration in the life of prayer.

While in Britain, I lived in a community where the prior, later to become a bishop in the Church of England, exemplified what it meant to be a person of prayer. He was the one who counselled that the only way to learn to pray was to pray! It was by living with him — by watching, listening and occasionally being able to walk together along quiet Somerset lanes and talk — that I began to understand what was happening in my relationship with the Cosmic Lover.

For some years, my soul friend was from another Christian community. While he was not in the ordained ministry, he was not unaware of the history of Christian spirituality. He was above all things a man of prayer, marked by a profound spiritual maturity, and he was not at all phased either by my differing tradition or by my theological training and ordination. He was very honest with me and, above all, being himself deeply connected to the Cosmic Lover in his own response to the adventure of prayer, truly carried me daily into the presence at the centre.

In another place and at a different stage of my journey, I was greatly helped to have an American priest as my spiritual director. He was well acquainted with the work of Carl Jung and had managed to integrate much of Jung's insights into what was, for me, a uniquely therapeutic path of spiritual friendship.

From different nations and Christian traditions, I have personally found spiritual guides — beloved 'midwives' — who have brought to birth so much of the life of the Spirit within me. I think you will understand now why I have reacted to Jahn and Magda in such a way.

As I have said, such guides are technically not necessary in the life of prayer. Having been raised up by the Cosmic Lover to facilitate the spiritual adventure, I believe that all on the journey should prayerfully seek to find a 'soul friend'.

The qualifications of a spiritual guide

Spiritual guides should obviously be personally integrated and mature. Above all, they should have had a long relationship in the life of prayer with the Cosmic Lover, travelled further into the heart of God, and be able to share freely and honestly from their own experience of uncertainty and struggle.

There should be no sense of being superior in those exercising this ministry. A soul friend is a sister or brother who is also a disciple, learning in humility about the life of prayer. They should have mastered the art of listening — listening to the story of the one who is seeking guidance, and also listening carefully for and discerning the direction of God in that story. Such ministries are found in response to a prayerful search and, when they are needed, God seems rarely to leave any seeker without such a ministry.

I am hoping that Jahn and Magda might be able to connect with a Christian guru for, while they have been many years on pilgrimage in a number of religious environments, they do not appear to have found a way that is personally fulfilling or connects them in any way personally with the divine. Perhaps a dinner party at the home of David and Jane might create a suitable milieu for further discussion. That's enough for now. See you on Thursday, I hope!

Alan

8

The unity of the body and spirit in prayer

Dear Peter,

In some recent conversations, both you and Pam have raised some important matters concerning how you perceive the Christian attitude to things material, particularly the body and the related issues of human sexuality. As we sat on the rocks in the Anakie Gorge some weeks back, you said that these things must have a bearing on the way we relate to God and therefore on the way we pray. I agree wholeheartedly!

Over the centuries, Christian thinking has not been immune from the influence of ideas dominant in the cultures in which Christians have lived. Perhaps uncritically, these have been absorbed and have coloured the way we have seen things. At times, they appear to have been embraced as an essential part of Christian belief. During the first centuries, Christians did not escape the grip of dualistic ideas. 'Dualism' describes the placing of things in two separate and incompatible categories.

One such dualism, which flowed from late Hellenistic Greek thinking, championed the 'soul' or 'spirit' as something essentially distinct from and superior to the 'body' or 'matter'. So some Christians began to believe that the way God wanted us to live involved suppressing all influence of the 'flesh' which was evil and embracing the realm of the 'spirit' which was good. The 'body' was temporal, material, earthy and subject to sickness and death, whereas the 'spirit' was permanent and immortal. As sexuality was so intimately associated with the 'flesh', at the least it was viewed with considerable suspicion.

This is a drastic separation of things that intrinsically belong together and I will take this up again a little later.

The sexist dualism within the Christian church

I have been helped in my thinking about these things by the writing of the American ethicist, James B. Nelson. He couples observations about dualism between body and spirit with what he terms *sexist or patriarchal dualism* — the systematic subordination

of women to men in Hebrew culture which profoundly influenced Christian thinking. Both spiritualistic and patriarchal dualisms, he writes, 'became
inextricably intertwined as men assumed to themselves superiority in spirit and reason while identi-
fying women with body, earthiness, irrationality
and instability'.[1]

From about the sixth century onwards, celibacy
was affirmed among many Christians as a superior
milieu in which the life of prayer could grow. The
way to communion with the divine was to focus on
the cultivation of the higher 'interior life' of the soul.
This involved a mortification of the body and of
sexual life which was associated with the 'lower
domain'.

I am not claiming that celibacy is in itself unhealthy or that those who choose to live celibate
lives have embraced an unhealthy dualism. The
great value in celibacy of harnessing the creativity
intrinsically connected to sexual energy can be seen
in many lives. While there is still quite a debate
going on in some circles, many Christians believe
that Jesus himself was most likely a celibate, as the
Gospels give no indication that he was married.

While there are hints of spirit-body dualism in
this quotation, and I risk being accused of inconsis-
tency in using it, I particularly like this description
of Gandhi's experience:

Deep in meditation, Gandhi began to see how much of his vital energy was locked up in the sexual drive. In a flood of insight, he realised that sex is not just a physical instinct, but an expression of the tremendous spiritual force behind all love and creativity which the Hindu scriptures call *kundalini*, the life-force of evolution. All his life it had been his master, buffeting him this way and that beyond his control. But in the silence of the Natal hills, with all his burning desire to serve focussed by weeks of tending to the wounded and dying, Gandhi found the strength to tap this power at its source. Then and there he resolved to be its master and never let it dictate to him again. It was a decision which resolved his deepest tensions and released all the love within him into his conscious control. He had begun to transform the last of his passions into spiritual power.[2]

There are many examples in the Christian story of the way in which celibates have channelled their sexual energies in noble and creative ways. The lives of most of these people do nothing to present as enemies the spiritual and the physical. Unhealthy distortions have prevailed when, coupled with the world view of dualistic divisions, celibacy has been given the status of a superior lifestyle.

Likewise, when the body and related sexuality is denounced as 'unspiritual' or inimical to the life of prayer or to proper living of the Christian faith, the holistic attitude affirming the unity of body and spirit has been severely compromised.

The movements of reform among Christians in sixteenth-century Europe, while questioning the superiority of celibacy, did little to change prevailing attitudes. The life of prayer and spiritual growth were both still largely separated from body and flesh and the leadership of the church continued to be overwhelmingly dominated by male attitudes.

As James B. Nelson notes:

> The idea that Christian spirituality might involve the celebration of one's flesh, the affirmation and healing of one's sexuality and an earthy, sensuous passion toward life was largely foreign.[3]

The Hebrew scriptures are undergirded by a belief in the created goodness of all being, and there have been times when Christians have advocated this understanding. There are aspects of the Christian scriptures which do not affirm sexist and spiritualistic dualisms. However, despite the declaration of the equality of all persons in Christ — 'neither Jew nor Greek. . . slave or free. . . male or female'[4] — contrary attitudes have often prevailed.

The incarnation of Jesus as affirmation of the unity of body and spirit

Crucial to this discussion is the belief central in Christian teaching of God's incarnation in human flesh. The test of orthodoxy from the earliest days was the conviction that Jesus Christ had come 'in the flesh'.[5] Because of this, there can be no dualism, no separation of things which rightly belong together. In the incarnation, spirit and flesh are united once more in complete integrity.

The apostle Paul's language about 'flesh' and 'spirit' is indicated in passages such as this from the Letter to the Romans:

> . . .those who live according to the flesh set their minds on the things of the flesh, but those who live according to the spirit set their minds on the things of the spirit. To set the mind on the flesh is death, but to set the mind on the spirit is life and peace.[6]

This has often led some to believe that to live truly as a Christian is to be more or less disembodied. A sharp dichotomy has been created between what is thought 'spiritual' and what is deemed 'ordinary'. In prayer, the discipline necessary to grow in relationship with the God who is Love is seen to necessitate a repression or mortification of the physical.

When we were talking last week, you mentioned your frustration when confronted with a text like this. You immediately took it that when the apostle Paul writes of 'flesh' in this way, it appears to undergird the Greek conception of the essential evil of matter, which prevailed in his day, and the consequent dichotomy between 'body' and 'spirit'.

However, when Paul is read in the context of all his writing, it becomes clear that he did not think in terms of Hellenistic dualism. For him, 'the flesh' did not refer to our bodies, but to that *interior disposition in humanity* which sets itself against relationship with God. The 'flesh' is grasping, ego-centred, constantly seeking to dominate and, as such, is divided and lacks integrity.

For the apostle Paul, to be 'spiritual' never meant to be disembodied. It meant having all things brought back into wholeness and integrity because they are in right relationship with God.

Christians believe that this occurs when one is united with the incarnate Jesus 'in whom the whole fullness of deity dwells bodily'.[7] The incarnation means that there can be no belittling of the body, or the physical and the material. Because it has been worn by God, our flesh is the most magnificent clothing of all. As well, Christians believe that Jesus did not discard our flesh at the end of his earthly ministry, like some garment no longer needed. In the ascension, our humanity in all of its fullness is taken into the life of the Trinity. To use the phrase from the wedding service: 'What God has joined together, let no-one put asunder.'

All this means that I will need some discernment in seeking to learn from my sisters and brothers in times past who wrote about the life of prayer. When I am confronted in their writing with an unhealthy dualism which negates the physical in order to advance the spiritual, I will reject it. I will not be afraid of a healthy sensuality which affirms the body and the material world, finding in the use of colour and smell, gesture and symbol a celebration of relationship with God which is anchored in the fabric of life.

American writer Thomas Howard puts it wonderfully:

> The incarnation took all that properly belongs to our humanity and delivered it back to us, redeemed. All of our inclinations and appetites and capacities and yearnings and proclivities are purified and gathered up and glorified by Christ. He did not come to thin our human life; he came to set it free. All the dancing and feasting and processing and singing and building and sculpting and baking and merrymaking that belong to us, and that were stolen away into the service of false gods, are returned to us in the gospel.[8]

The link between prayer and sexuality

I still laugh about Pam's story of 'Lydia the Astounding' which she related during that wonderful afternoon under the Moreton Bay fig, after the meal we had at the 'Fisherman's Net'. She is understandably not particularly enthusiastic about what she perceives to be the 'unhealthy attitudes' which Christians allegedly perpetuate about sexuality. I know from subsequent conversations that you have similar opinions.

Because it is related to what I have been saying about unhelpful dualisms, I want to share my reflections about a poem that I have recently 'rediscovered'. I have been discussing it with James and Tricia as part of their marriage preparation.

The Australian poet James McAuley came into focus again last week in a television program concerning his involvement with Harold Stewart in writing the 'Ern Malley' poems. This was a marvellous hoax. The two colleagues concocted verses made up of haphazard words and phrases from a chance assortment of books — all in the name of an imaginary deceased poet, Ern Malley. The poems were sent off to a literary journal and, in due course, were warmly embraced as the work of a major poet. The two mavericks succeeded in sending up the literary establishment in the mid-1940s.

McAuley also wrote a host of his own serious poetry. 'Nuptial Hymn' is among my favourites. It is alive with biblical and liturgical imagery and presents the act of sexual love not only as communion between two human beings, but as a prayer which the earth shares through their rapture. This is a uniquely evocative image of human sexuality which I believe to be both wholesome and Christian!

> *The thick candle with the golden flame*
> Dipped in the womb of waters — holy rite —
> Quenchless has quickened it with secret light;
> The dead have risen; seraphs sing the Name,
> Which is an oil poured forth upon the night.
>
> Come, flesh redeemed, with chrism of joy anointed,
> The children of the Spirit and the Bride,
> God's breathing icons: naked, side by side,
> Enter the paradise for you appointed;
> The cherub's sword shall guard you, not divide.
>
> From your embrace in flower honey is stored
> By spirits clustering in the eternal comb;
> Expectant earth beneath the starry dome
> Sings through your bodies' rapture to its Lord:
> O Lumen Christi, leading all things home.[9]

I should let the poem with its powerful imagery speak for itself, but I can't resist the temptation to prattle on a bit about how I see it.

The first verse evokes images of the ancient Easter vigil when Christians renew their baptismal covenant with the Cosmic Lover, a covenant of renewed life and love and light overcoming darkness. New life has been created, alluded to by the phallic candle, the symbol of the Risen Christ, dipped into the waters of the womb-like baptismal font. Its light is not able to be quenched. The oil which anoints new Christians in baptism has the fragrance of love suggested in 'the oil poured forth' — a reference to the celebration of human sexuality at the beginning of Solomon's Song of Songs.[10]

The children of the Spirit and the Bride have joyfully been restored to Paradise their ancient home, integrated in their relationship with God. Not like the painted icons which are claimed to bear the likeness of the person they image, they are 'God's breathing icons'. In their redeemed flesh, they reflect the image and likeness of their Creator: naked, side by side, no longer divided, no longer ashamed in their disintegration, no longer needing to hide behind the loincloths of fig leaves,[11] they are reinstated in their rightful place. The cherubim and the sword which cast them out of Eden and caused them to be aliens have now become their guardians.

The embrace of the lovers and the orgasmic bodily celebration of their love is their prayer, their communion with the Cosmic Lover. They, and the earth with them, rapturously sing to God who in Jesus leads all things home.

The apostle Paul in his letter to the Ephesians writes of the love between two human beings in the covenant of marriage being an icon of the love between Jesus and his people. This is a 'mystery'[12]or sign for us to contemplate and discover in the experience of human love.

In the First Letter of John, there are some more challenging sentences about the relationship between human love and experiencing God. Here, traditionally the word translated as 'love' has been interpreted as 'spiritual' and disembodied and, as a consequence, loses much of its significance. When we read it as giving 'love' its broad and wholesome meaning, we capture something of its power:

> Beloved, let us love one another, because love is from God; everyone who loves is born of God and knows God. Whoever does not love does not know God, for God is love... No-one has ever seen God; if we love one another, God lives in us and God's love is perfected in us... God is love, and those who abide in love abide in God and God abides in them.[13]

It has only been in the experience of human love in all of its wonderful facets of physical celebration and spiritual discovery that I have been able to grasp, in terms that I can understand, the encounter I have with the Cosmic Lover in prayer. In the silence of encounter with God, where 'my idea of myself... has to be shattered time after time', I grow in a robust acceptance of my sexuality and, liberated, I begin to appreciate it from God's perspective. I believe that when Christians can be seen to embrace the wholesome attitudes to the celebration of human sexuality which are inherent in the Gospel, it might help others to seek for an encounter with the Cosmic Lover who has created them and, through the adventure of the life of prayer, enter into the lovingly rapturous life of the Trinity.

I hope it will not be long before we have another gathering with Sue and Pam when we can throw around some of these ideas — and perhaps lessen some of the clout in Pam's ammunition! As you are to be in Perth for a few weeks, it will probably not be until after the wedding of Tricia and James that we will be able to indulge in another long lunch! And you wanted me to write about fasting! That will have to wait for another letter.

Watch out the quokkas don't get you on Rottnest Island!

Alan

9

The experience of fasting and prayer

Dear Peter,

It is all very quiet here as you are not the only one away. There are few friends around with whom to indulge in the culinary delights of our usual haunts. You may well think it an appropriate environment for my writing about prayer and *fasting*!

I should say at the outset that fasting in the context of the life of prayer has little connection with dieting, losing weight or the body shape of those who claim to find it beneficial. It is not the hunger strike which is sometimes practised as a political protest.

These are not in themselves wrong. In a Christian context, however, they are simply not what fasting is about. Fasting is not an example of that harmful body-versus-spirit dualism of which I wrote in my last letter, which flourished particularly during the Middle Ages in excesses of bodily mortification. It is not religious masochism!

What fasting is

Fasting is usually thought of as an abstinence from food. There can be other kinds of fasting, however, with which I have had little or no association, but which have become part of the discipline which Christians practise as part of their life of prayer.

Some find it helpful to fast from radio, television and the telephone for a period, not because they are wrong in themselves, but so that they have a more focussed and undistracted time with the Cosmic Lover. Others fast from family and friends (some even from sexual relationships with their partners) to spend some time in solitude perhaps in another place so that they might be more in tune with God at the centre.

What the purpose of fasting is

Fasting, though not unique to the Christian tradition, has been part of the Christian way of prayer from the beginning. In the teaching of Jesus, there is a clear assumption that fasting is not an option. In the context of the Sermon on the Mount, Jesus said '*when* you fast', not '*if* you fast'.

Jesus in that context is concerned to denounce all

outward manifestations of fasting which would turn the practice into some religious self-display. It is concerned about the private and personal relationship of the beloved and the Cosmic Lover.

In the life and teaching of Jesus, fasting seems to be associated with times of intense prayer. Before Jesus commenced his public ministry, he fasted and prayed for some forty days. This was also a time of confrontation with some alternative and spectacular ways of carrying out his mission which would have been in the end compromises with evil. The intensity of the fasting may have sharpened Jesus' discernment during such a trial.

In the Acts of the Apostles, fasting is associated with prayer that seeks discernment concerning the appointment of new leaders in the Christian community or the commencement of a new work. Fasting appears to be part of a time of fervent concentration in prayer.

Fasting in Christian practice is not an exercise in magic. I have known some Christians to fast with the seeming motive of making God more aware of something, to cause a change in what is perceived to be the divine purpose, or to achieve some special boon or blessing. I have even had to endure sermons which extolled the blessings which would automatically follow if fasting were observed. God was made out to be something easily manipulated by a fast —

much like a gambling machine which produced the jackpot when the right numbers were inserted. This gives wonderful fuel for radio commentator Terry Lane's writing about God!

Unfortunately, I have had to experience prayer groups which approached fasting like a child in the supermarket demanding an ice cream. It performs a dramatic tantrum and then holds its breath until the frustrated parent relents. That is not what fasting is about. God is not like some reluctant miser who needs to be treated in such a way.

Peter, you will not be surprised that there have been conflicts among Christians over the merits of fasting. Some have claimed that by fasting there could be obtained special favours from God such as respite from certain purgatorial experiences in the afterlife. Some rejected such notions, denying the meritorious quality of the practice and questioning its validity. Thus, fasting has had little place among the people of that tradition. Others, while also reacting against what they believed to be unwholesome reasons for fasting, still commended it as a vital part of the life of prayer.

I believe that fasting is meant to be practised simply for God's sake. There may be secondary purposes which are of great benefit but, from the outset, the Christian fasts as an act of love — to focus more specifically on the person of the Cosmic Lover.

If this is not so and other motives distract, it ceases to be part of the response of prayer and the whole exercise loses its chief concern. As such, it fails. It was John Wesley (who took the spiritual disciplines in my own Christian community so seriously that he was thought very odd and nicknamed a 'Methodist') who wrote concerning fasting: 'First, let it be done unto the Lord with our eye singly fixed on him. Let our intention herein be this and this alone. . .'[1]

There are other reasons for fasting which are not at the heart of my own practice of fasting. Some fast because it is a virtual tangible expression of their hunger for God and an indication of their desire to cooperate with God's purposes in their lives. I have to admit to finding that kind of attitude doesn't quite fit my personality. Nor do I readily identify with those who fast to counter the sin of gluttony (I can just hear you making all kinds of rude and pointed remarks over that one!).

Some Christians fast in order to express repentance and to mark a change in their lives that is more clearly God-centred. If this is not a wallowing in unhealthy guilt, but a vital part of the growing relationship of love between the Cosmic Lover and one being invited to respond, then there can be no question of its appropriateness.

How fasting benefits prayer

Those who regularly practise fasting from food witness to the way in which it intensifies and concentrates the experience of prayer. I have found that to try to pray after a meal presents me with considerable difficulty. My body is centred on digestion and I can become quite drowsy. When I am fasting, I am much more alert, seemingly more sensitive to the voice of God at the centre and better able to respond in the personal battle which sometimes happens in becoming the person God intends that I be.

(Remember: 'my idea of myself is not a divine idea — it needs to be shattered time after time'!)

It is during a period of fasting that I am more often able, as the Cosmic Lover sensitively directs, to confront the negative aspects in my unconscious which come to the surface during these periods. Personal fasts are for me largely responses made in the encounters I have with God at the centre. Consequently, there is no regular pattern or specific discipline in those fasts — they are just a matter between God and myself.

How communal fasting benefits prayer

Christians have often set aside periods for fasting together. This has ranged from the more spontaneous communal decisions of small contemporary fellowship groups to the formal set days of the ancient churches.

I have been greatly helped in my spiritual journey by the rhythm of fasting and feasting which makes up the traditional Christian year. The celebration of Easter has almost from the earliest times been preceded by a period of fasting. In the West, this has evolved into a period of forty days (Sundays are always feast days and are excluded!). Originally, Easter was a time for the baptism and reception into the Christian community of new converts.

Prayer and fasting was part of the preparation for baptism and it soon became the practice for the rest of the Christian community to join the candidates for baptism in this discipline. This period is what we know in the West as *Lent* (which took its name from an ancient English word for Spring — the season in the northern hemisphere during which it was held). It became a time of intensified prayer and spiritual renewal for the whole Christian community — and there is nothing like a fast to make a feast even more celebratory!

I greatly value Lent. Like many of my contemporaries, it is not now a time for the traditional abstention from a lot of food. It is primarily a time for intensification of prayer and the making of more space for growth in relationship with the Cosmic Lover. At times for me, this has meant spending an hour less each night in sleep so that the time can be spent with God. Coupled with this might be a refraining from meat or visits to the cinema or the theatre — just to keep the purpose of the season at the forefront of my attention. Doing this with fellow Christians helps to give a greater focus to the purposes of Lent and generally this has been a positive part of my journey.

While I was part of a monastic community in the West Country of England, Lent was something I found dreadful. Other brothers and sisters might have gained a great deal and grown in their relationship with God considerably. I had not been part of any tradition which observed Lent with any great severity. There were extra penitential psalms said each day in the chapel which seemed to make the long periods of prayer even longer. It did not seem to make me more given to personal prayer. I think I was going through a period in my journey with God which was not one that I can recall as greatly felicitous.

At breakfast, coarse and often stale wholemeal bread was all that was provided and this was not to be toasted. A rather unpalatable English cooking margarine was all that was available to add to it and, as I tried to digest it with strong black tea, I tried in vain to find ways to relate this to positive growth in the spiritual journey.

I can remember feelings of respite and minor indulgence in the middle of Lent when an English pound note, sent in a letter from my father in Australia, was spent on a chocolate bar at the village shop. Perhaps I am just not temperamentally suited to this kind of spirituality and this may be at the basis of my suspicion of what we have sometimes facetiously termed 'barbed-wire underwear' Christianity.

A period of fasting and preparation for some four weeks leading to the celebration of Christmas known as *Advent* — similar to, but perhaps not as severe as Lent — is also officially observed as a fast among Christians in my own tradition. This is a difficult communal fast to observe because in Australia the month before Christmas is marked by end-of-year parties and all kinds of festivities often labelled as 'Christmas parties' for social groups, friends, families and office groups. Many come to the feast of Christmas, having sung carols and Christmas songs for weeks, exhausted, over-fed and somewhat jaded by all that has led up to it.

I sometimes wish that the northern hemisphere celebration of the solstice, which we Christians tried to 'baptise', we could quietly 'unbaptise' and find another time during which we could celebrate the birth of Jesus.

Wednesdays and Fridays (because Friday was the day of the crucifixion of Jesus) have been traditionally set aside in my own tradition as days of fasting and abstinence. These have been observed over the years with either total disregard or with genuine seriousness. While a member of the Somerset community, 'Friday fare' consisted of an evening meal of mashed potato, sprinkled with a few peanuts. Rarely did this practice prove beneficial to my relationship with the Cosmic Lover, although for my more dedicated and fervent brothers and sisters, this may well have been of immense value.

In another situation, I found the skipping of lunch and the opportunity to go to chapel at the ringing of a bell at three on a Friday afternoon for some silence and centring prayer a much more beneficial practice.

Well, my friend, you will gather that I am not the greatest advocate or exponent of the practice of fasting as part of the life of prayer. It only has value for me when it is totally to do with my relationship with God and, when orchestrated by God, its purposes become obvious. I *never* fast for fasting's sake, and I never associate fasting with weight reduction, fasting for other health purposes, or fasting for supposedly 'spiritual' consciousness-raising as directly part of the Christian way of prayer.

Nevertheless I do not think anyone can take the Christian spiritual journey seriously without fasting from time to time.

The next time we meet will be at the wedding of Tricia and James. Knowing the way David and Jane are preparing, it will hardly be an occasion for fasting! It will be a wonderful time of joyful celebration and I am really glad to have been asked to celebrate the marriage. See you then.

With warmest regards as always,

Alan

10

'The dark night of the soul'

Dear Peter,
I am delighted to see your prejudices challenged! Is it really so incredible that a small wedding celebration chiefly among Christians should be such a magnificent occasion? It was a great opportunity for the friends of James and Tricia to demonstrate their considerable creativity.

I am sure that the Head of the Drama Department would have been most impressed with the way John and Megan presented the readings from the Song of Songs. They steered a careful course between an unseemly eroticism and an over-chaste misrepresentation of the biblical material and thus sensitively captured its depiction of the sensuous delight of the bodily celebration of human love. That is why it had such a powerful and moving effect on all who were present and 'shocked' you in the best possible way!

I gather that 'Set me as a seal on your heart' — which Philip composed for the occasion — was given quite an accolade when performed by the Chorale at the Faculty concert on Monday night. And Jane and David in their own unique way crowned the day with their superlative catering and wonderful hospitality.

I am very happy for Tricia and James. As you know, with all the difficulties in their families, the way to the day of their wedding has not been easy and there will be nothing fairy-tale about the next few years, but it was great to be able to encourage them by putting our best efforts into creating a 'wow!' celebration of their marriage. They deserve it!

But then I am not writing to wax eloquent about wedding celebrations. You have asked for more fodder for our dialogue about the life of prayer — and so on with the task!

As you know for some time now, the first part of Thursday mornings at home has been given over to meeting with a group of students who are preparing for ministry in the Christian community. They come at seven for about three-quarters-of-an-hour of centring prayer in silence and then, over breakfast, there is much lively discussion before they have to appear at lectures. I have learned a considerable amount during these times. In recent weeks, discussions have centred around the experience of what was termed 'dryness of spirit' or, to use the phrase which originated with the Spanish mystic St John of the Cross, the 'dark night of the soul'.

Wrong explanations when God seems far away

A couple of weeks ago, there was a lot of laughter at the breakfast table about those dreadful car stickers propagating gauche religious slogans. One which went *'If God seems far away ---- who moved?'* prompted what has become one of the lengthiest and most profound periods of dialogue we have had since we began.

David, a bright final year student, shared that he had been going through a long period during which he had felt abandoned by God. He had lost all sense of the presence of God, particularly during his specific times of 'centring'. All the 'disciplines' which had up to this period been helpful in encountering God had become merely mechanical and, because they bore no fruit, became burdensome.

That car sticker had caused him some concern. In his experience, God *did* seem far away. Consequently, he had descended into a black hole of introspection looking for some wrong turning in the spiritual journey or some fault he had unwittingly embraced. From some personal discussions and by the fruits of his life, I knew that David had not 'moved'. These students were not just beginners in the life of prayer, so I was not all that surprised when one of the women said: 'You are always reminding us that, essentially, prayer is *not* our activity. It is *God's* activity in us. Now, if David has been experiencing the seeming absence of God, what is God doing?'

As you can imagine, this brought on quite a discussion!

There were some who thought that the problem was not with God, but with David. There were suggestions about some 'hidden' aspect of David's journey which may have caused a serious breach in his relationship with God. Allusions were made to biblical passages which seemed to imply that the 'hiding of the face of God' was the experience of those who strayed from the path God intends for us. Of course, this was a selective drawing on biblical texts, but the real issue soon surfaced.

There seemed to be a need to comprehend David's experience in terms of wrongdoing. If David had not done anything wrong, it meant that blame shifted from David to God — and they could not cope with such a possibility. God needed to be defended and it could only be done by making David a candidate for a resurrected Inquisition!

Others suggested that if David had not moved, then God was capricious. We had come to understand God as the Cosmic Lover who longed for relationship with humankind and pursued us until we entered into the loving embrace of God we know to be prayer. If, having experienced God in that way, God moved away, it was most unfair. Doubt was placed on God being the God of unconditional love. Love (which seemed to be equated with the sense of the presence of God) seemed to be being used by God as a manipulative instrument and, in so doing, God was no better than an inadequate parent!

Another possibility was raised. David was asked about his lifestyle. The possibility of mental or physical fatigue was canvassed. Perhaps he was trying to tackle too much in his studies. If this were so, it might have led to the feeling that God was far away. David assured us that this was not a reflection of his experience.

Someone asked whether an encounter with God the Cosmic Lover meant that prayer was meant to be equated with something like the delights of an 'Arabian Nights'-type fantasy. Perhaps our idea of *prayer* was not a divine idea — it needed to be shattered time after time, to slightly misquote C.S. Lewis.

Returning to the assumption that all this was part

of God's activity in us, we again asked: 'What is God doing?'

Our early experiences of prayer: a love based on the senses

From both my experience of the life of prayer and my reading of those who in the past have been fellow travellers, there appears to be a pattern of growth in our encounter with the God who calls us into relationship.

This firstly involves that initial response when we first begin to experience God in the life of prayer. This might best be described as growth in the *knowledge* of God (and also, as we have discussed, about ourselves). It is that period when we first begin to experience C.S. Lewis's axiom: 'My idea of God is not a divine idea; it has to be shattered time after time.'

There is a sense in which we never cease growing in our knowledge of God. But out of the initial growth in knowledge will come growth in the *love* of God. This has been described by some of the masters as a movement from the head to the heart. Prayer becomes predominantly expressive of an affective response to the Cosmic Lover rather than a concentration on the reflective.

Leonard Boase writes of it like this:

We reach a saturation-point in our absorbing the truth of God's revelation. Our sponge is full; there is more water left in the ocean, but we have absorbed what we need. Discovery and exploration are no longer such a pleasure; what we seek is to enjoy what we have attained.[1]

In time, God will move us away from that environment in which our senses are paramount. We will learn that our relationship with God cannot be adequately evaluated by how we feel.

A particular time spent in centring prayer may have produced a desired outcome accompanied by positive emotional responses. We sense the presence of God and we enjoy the feeling. There has been some fruitful dialogue and we have been deeply affirmed. Prayer has been easy and full of considerable comfort. We think of that as a 'good' prayer time.

Another person may have been littered with frustrating distractions without any sense of connectedness with God. There has been some difficult or painful confrontation and so we evaluate that period as a 'bad' prayer time.

What we assess to be a 'good' time, from the divine perspective, may be no such thing. Conversely, what we have thought of as a 'bad' time may well have accomplished a great deal. The value of our encounters with God are not measured by the way we feel. The marks of an authentic life of prayer are not found in experience of good feelings, but in growth in the likeness of God. The apostle John writes of this in his First Letter:

> Those who say, 'I love God,' and hate their brothers and sisters, are liars; for those who do not love a brother or sister whom they have seen, cannot love God whom they have not seen.[2]

Often, in conjunction with this 'bad' time, we will experience a sense of abandonment by God when we experience God's work of shattering false images. Having moved from one image of God to another, each time seeing that God is *not* the image, we come to a point when we are confronted with the loss of the image as the loss of God. This can be a time of great insecurity and I have known some to give up prayer at this point as a forlorn exercise.

Our later experience of prayer: a love beyond the senses

It is very important to grasp that God will lead us to pray centred very much in the senses, before we will be led to any other kind of experience of the life of prayer. But as we move 'beyond the beginnings' of the life of prayer, there will come a time when God will lead us deliberately into an experience of the loss of God.

It is not that we have moved away from God. It is not the result of straying from God's path. It is not a time of image shattering. It is not attributable to fatigue or some other explicable cause. The journey to this point has caused us to associate the modes by which we experience God with the reality of God. The senses which have been fired by the use of our minds, imaginations and affections in response to the Cosmic Lover will cease to be of help. They are, if you like, crutches which have helped us to walk with God.

In the end, however, we have to learn that God is not to be identified with any of these things. It is as if God is saying to us: 'Do you love me for myself or because you experience joy and comfort in our relationship? If I were to remove the experience of joy and comfort, would you still remain faithful?'

Initially, it seems to be cruel to have been seduced into a relationship with the Cosmic Lover, only seemingly to be abandoned at the time when we have become profoundly connected with God. Yet God does this! I have seen it happen to many who have shared with me their spiritual journey. I warm to the story attributed to Teresa of Avila who complained to God that it was no wonder that God had so few friends considering the way God treated those few friends!

In the end, God will teach the one who perseveres

that what was thought to be love was not love at all. We do not enter into relationship with God for our own gratification, even though the initial attraction to God was pleasurable. Having all the props removed, we are then confronted with the challenge to faithfulness, to embrace the *will* to love God in the darkness, to hold on to the reality of God when there is nothing in the senses to assure us of God's presence.

This, I guess, is what faith is about. Once we have gone beyond the panic and the sense of abandonment, we can embrace the experience of 'dryness' as normal in the life of prayer. Paradoxically, this 'dark night of the senses' is the place of inner transformation and the most spiritual growth. The hardest lesson during this period is to learn to do nothing and let what God intends be accomplished.

I have seen many respond to this time by trying to fill the emptiness with all kinds of activity. They take on some different way of meditation from another tradition, or investigate another kind of spirituality, in the hope that they can rekindle their initial experiences of prayer. Others give up the inner journey altogether and become very busy in religious work or the pursuit of biblical knowledge.

The reaction is understandable. I believe that God lovingly grieves for them, as paradoxically they have embraced a meagre substitute for the great things God would accomplish in them if they would simply let go and do nothing.

If they would but do so, God works a great transformation within. This, however, is according to God's own timing and according to the divine agenda as God truly knows what is best for us.

John of the Cross and 'the dark night of the soul'

As you know, Peter, John of the Cross, the sixteenth-century Spanish mystic, has long been one of my mentors. There is much which I find difficult in the typically intense scholastic style of his day, but there is great treasure in his writing. Even in translation, the poetry of this Castilian I find wonderfully incisive and encouraging for the spiritual journey.

John uses the image of a log becoming fire to describe what God is doing during this time of darkness. At first, God's love like fire 'turns the wood black and makes it dark. . .'[3] This parallels with the darkening of the senses. As the heat penetrates into the heart of the log, it transforms the substance of the wood until the it becomes fire.

The image of burning is fascinating, because before this process is complete, things don't appear very nice. The procedure is not without its pain and struggle, and it is very easy to lose one's nerve while it is going on. No-one, as far as I am aware, has encountered this experience with ease. It is a time when a wise mentor can be a great help. But because it is essentially God's business, and one in which God's love is at work within us, the end explains the process.

John of the Cross uses the image of the burning love of God and beautifully develops it in his poem, *Living Flame of Love*. This is one of the pieces of writing I use in my praying when things are a bit grim, yet I sense that God is nevertheless at work within. In this context, I find that it takes on a wonderfully passionate and gentle character and somehow rests in a more tolerable milieu:

> Oh, living flame of love
> That tenderly woundest my soul in its deepest centre,
> Since thou art no longer oppressive, perfect me now if it
> be thy will,
> Break the web of this sweet encounter.
> Oh, sweet burn! Oh delectable wound!
> Oh, soft hand! Oh, delicate touch
> That savours of eternal life and pays every debt!
> In slaying, thou hast changed death into life.
> Oh lamps of fire, in whose splendours
> The deep caverns of sense
> Which were dark and blind with strange brightness
> Give heat and light together to their Beloved!

I think that will have to do for now. The 'long lunch' we have been threatening for weeks has not yet happened, so let's meet again at the 'Windmill' early next week to catch up with all that has been going on.

With warmest regards as always,

Alan

Postscript

Dear Peter,

The menu at the 'Windmill' yesterday was exceptional. A couple of hours to catch up with all that has been happening with you no doubt enhanced my perceptions.

The things I have shared in my letters over the past weeks have been attempts to respond to your request to put on paper some of the things about prayer we have discussed in our meetings together and gatherings with others. You will realise that they are hardly an exhaustive compendium on a Christian understanding about prayer. They are an attempt to share something of the way of prayer as I have experienced it and my reflections on some of the issues which have to be faced as one continues on the journey.

Yesterday you asked where you should go from here. I can only repeat the counsel I received from one of my mentors. The only way to learn how to pray is to pray! God the Cosmic Lover has created us for that relationship we call prayer. It is God who is the source of that longing, which leads us to seek that relationship.

The words of Jesus have some relevance to this:

> Ask, and it will be given you; search, and you will find, knock, and the door will be opened for you. For everyone who asks receives, and everyone who searches finds, and for everyone who knocks, the door will be opened.[1]

Asking, searching and knocking are what this relationship with the Cosmic Lover is all about. It is a matter of heart to heart — the heart of God seeking and finding union with the human heart.

I appreciate what you have shared with me about your own responses. May your fascination with the possibilities of the spiritual journey continue to grow and may your experience of the Love which holds the universe together bring profound satisfaction in the depths of your being.

With my warmest regards,

Alan

Endnotes

Introduction
1. Julian of Norwich, *Showings*, Classics of Western Spirituality, Paulist Press, 1978, pp.342 and 343
2. T.S. Eliot, 'Little Gidding', in *Four Quartets*, Faber and Faber, 1953, p.36

Chapter 1
1. *The Collected Works of C.G. Jung*, Sir Herbert Read, et al (eds), R.F.C. Hull (trans.), Princeton University Press, 1969, VIII, p.158
2. *Op.cit.*, XI, pp.109-200
3. *Ibid*, p.193
4. Francis Thompson, *The Hound of Heaven* in R.S. Thomas (ed.), The Penguin Book of Religious Verse, Penguin Books, Harmondsworth, Middlesex, 1963, p.32
5. Holy Sonnet XVII, in *John Donne*, J. Hayward (ed.), Penguin, 1950, p.172
6. *An Australian Prayer Book*, AIO, 1978, p.146
7. St Bonaventure, Major Life of St Francis, in M.A. Habig,

St Francis of Assisi Writings and Early Biographies, Franciscan Herald Press, 1973, p.695

8. 'God's Grandeur', in The Poems of Gerard Manley Hopkins, R. Bridges and W.H. Gardner (eds), Oxford University Press, 1960, p.70

9. An Australian Prayer Book, AIO, 1978, pp.61 and 62

Chapter 2

1. 1 John 4, verses 9 and 10
2. Acts 17, verse 28
3. See M. Basil Pennington, O.S.C.O., Centering Prayer, Doubleday, 1980
4. Matthew 6, verse 6
5. See Mark 1, verse 35
6. Henri J.M. Nouwen, The Way of the Heart, Darton, Longman and Todd, 1981, p.43
7. C.S. Lewis, A Grief Observed, Seabury Press, New York, 1961, p.52

Chapter 3

1. T.S. Eliot, 'Little Gidding', in Four Quartets, Faber and Faber, 1953, p.36
2. Carl Jung, Collected Works, XII, p.11, Footnote 6
3. See Romans 8, verses 26 and 27

Chapter 4

1. Hebrews 4, verse 12
2. Luke 9, verses 51 to 56
3. Psalm 27, verse 1, An Australian Prayer Book, AIO, 1978, p.334
4. The Service for Wednesday Evening, An Australian Prayer Book, AIO, 1978, p.70
5. In Gerard W. Hughes, God of Surprises, Darton,

Longman and Todd, 1985, p.53

6. John 4, verses 4 to 30
7. *Australian Hymn Book*, Collins, Sydney, 1977, No.335
8. See John 16, verses 12 and 13

Chapter 5

1. Terry Lane: *God: The Interview*, ABC Books, 1993, pp.72 and 73
2. *Ibid*
3. Luke 12, verses 6 and 7
4. Revelation 13, verses 1 to 3
5. C.S. Lewis, *The Magician's Nephew*, Penguin, 1963, pp.131 and 132
6. Nikos Kazantzakis, *Report To Greco*, Simon and Schuster, New York, 1965, p.305
7. Daniel Berrigan, *America is Hard to Find*, SPCK, 1973, pp.77 and 78
8. Matthew 25, verses 35 to 40
9. Exodus 3, verses 1 to 6
10. Joan Puls, *Every Bush is Burning*, World Council of Churches, Geneva, 1987

Chapter 6

1. 1 Corinthians 12, verse 27
2. Acts 2, verses 42 and 46
3. Psalm 104, verses 25 to 30, translation in Joseph Gelineau, *The Psalms: A New Translation*, Collins, 1965
4. Psalm 63, verse 1, Joseph Gelineau, *op.cit.*
5. Psalm 55, verses 12 to 21, extracts from Joseph Gelineau, *op.cit.*
6. Psalm 55, verse 15, Joseph Gelineau, *op.cit.*
7. Psalm 137, verses 8 and 9, *Australian Prayer Book* version, *italics mine*

8. Psalm 91, extracts from verses 1 to 10
9. 1 Corinthians 12, verse 26

Chapter 7

1. I have found this term to be most apt in describing the role of the 'spiritual guide'. I heard it first used by Professor Margaret Guenther during a course of lectures she gave at Wollaston College, Perth. She has a chapter entitled 'The Spiritual Director as Midwife' in her book *Holy Listening*, Darton, Longman and Todd, 1992

2. See *The Sayings of the Desert Fathers*, Benedicta Ward SLG (trans.), Mowbray, 1981

   There are some of the sayings of ammas like Theodora, Sarah and Syncletica contained in this collection, but the work largely reflects the sayings of the abbas. This does not necessarily imply that the presence of ammas was minimal. It may have more to do with attitudes concerning men and women which prevailed at the time of the compilation of the *Apophthegmata*.

3. Richard Foster, *The Celebration of Discipline*, Hodder and Stoughton, 1984, p.245

4. John Chryssavgis, *The Spiritual Father As Embodiment of Tradition*, in *Phronema* (St. Andrews Greek Orthodox Theological College, Sydney), Vol.1, 1986, p.20

5. James Walsh, in *The Way*, Vol.2, No.3, 1962, p.208

6. Michael Hollings in Sheila Cassidy's *Prayer for Pilgrims*, Fount, 1980, p.10

Chapter 8

1. James B. Nelson, *Between Two Gardens*, Pilgrim Press, 1983, p.7

2. Eknath Easwaran, *Gandhi, the Man*, Blue Mountain Center of Meditation, Berkeley, 1972, pp.37 and 38

3. James B. Nelson, *The Intimate Connection*, Westminster, 1988, p.23
4. Galatians 3, verse 28
5. 1 John 4, verse 2
6. Romans 8, verses 5 and 6
7. Colossians 2, verse 9
8. Thomas Howard, *Evangelical Is Not Enough*, Nelson, 1984, pp.36 and 37
9. James McAuley, *Collected Poems 1936--1970*, Angus and Robertson, Sydney 1971
10. Song of Songs, 1, verses 2 and 3
11. Genesis 2, verse 25 and chapter 3, verse 7
12. Ephesians 5, verse 32
13. 1 John 4, verses 7, 12 and 16

Chapter 9

1. John Wesley, *Sermons on Several Occasions*, Epworth Press, 1971, p.301

Chapter 10

1. Leonard Boase S.J., *The Prayer of Faith*, Darton, Longman and Todd, 1976, p.67
2. 1 John 4, verse 20
3. *The Dark Night*, Book II, Chapter 10 1, in *The Collected Works of St John of the Cross*, Kieran Kavanagh and Otilio Rodriguez (trans.), ICS Publications, 1973, p.350

Postscript

1. Luke 11, verses 9 and 10

Bibliography

AN ANCIENT PROVERB CLAIMS that 'of making many books there is no end', and one could add that this is specially so with books on the life of prayer. I have tried to make a brief bibliography of some of the writings which have influenced my understanding, fed my experience and enabled me to journey with the Cosmic Lover with a little more integrity than otherwise might have been the case.

□ Anthony Bloom, *Living Prayer*, Darton, Longman and Todd, 1966
Russian Orthodox Archbishop Anthony (Anthony Bloom) introduced me to the special insights of Eastern Christians, particularly the place of silence and listening in our journey with the Cosmic Lover.

☐ Leonard Boase, *The Prayer of Faith*, Darton, Longman and Todd, 1976

Jesuit Leonard Boase first wrote this classic in the 1940s and has rewritten it for a more contemporary readership. A good book for thinking beginners in the life of prayer, it is well grounded in the realities of the human journey and gives reassurance to those for whom the way is not easy.

☐ Christopher Bryant, *The River Within*, Darton, Longman and Todd, 1978

The river of life deep within us carries us through the stages of our life with the Cosmic Lover. Bryant uses this powerful image to colour his helpful insights into meditation and contemplative prayer.

☐ Sheila Cassidy, *Prayer for Pilgrims*, Fount, 1980

In this account of her work as a doctor among the destitute in Chile, the author gives an excellent introduction to the life of prayer which has been forged through personal suffering in her search for renewal of faith.

☐ Graeme Davidson, *Anyone Can Pray*, Paulist, 1983

Davidson and coauthor Mary Macdonald bring together prayer forms drawn from Anglican, Orthodox, Protestant and Roman Catholic traditions. It is a basic work for those who are beginners, but those a little further along the way will find enrichment in its breadth of scope.

☐ Gerard Hughes, *God of Surprises*, Darton, Longman and Todd, 1985

Insightful, wise and specially written for those disillusioned by institutional religion, Hughes writes of surprising encounters with the Cosmic Lover who will not be domesticated by our false images and dogmatic securities.

☐ Morton Kelsey, *The Other Side of Silence*, Paulist, 1976

Kelsey writes specially for those who have turned to the Eastern religions for help in learning about meditation. He makes a strong claim for the Christian tradition of meditation which many in the West did not know existed or had neglected.

☐ Kenneth Leech, *True Prayer*, Sheldon Press, 1980

Leech assumes little prior knowledge of the Christian way of prayer and writes for the thinking person who is willing to explore the journey with the Cosmic Lover.

☐ George Maloney, *Inward Stillness*, Dimension Books, 1975

☐ George Maloney, *Prayer of the Heart*, Ave Maria Press, 1980

Maloney brings a profound understanding and experience of prayer from both the Eastern and Western Christian heritage. *Inward Stillness* explores the place of silence in discovering the divine. *Prayer of the Heart* is an interpretation for the Western mind of that tradition of the Jesus Prayer. Among his many books, these two have had considerable influence on my own experience of the journey.

☐ Mary Clare, *Encountering the Depths*, Darton, Longman and Todd,1981

Mary Clare is a member of an Anglican contemplative community in Oxford, England, and has had a long ministry as a spiritual guide. Her writings are simple yet profound in their insights. I read this book in the early stages of my journey with the Cosmic Lover and still find new insights when I return to it.

☐ Julian of Norwich, *Showings*, Classics of Western Spirituality, Paulist, 1978

This is a new translation of the writing of this fourteenth century mystic. People seeking writing from the perspective of a woman of prayer are finding that this classic has much to say at the end of this millennium about life with the Cosmic Lover.

☐ Henri Nouwen, *The Way of the Heart*, Darton, Longman and Todd, 1981

This prolific author is probably one of the significant teachers of the way of prayer. Nouwen here gives an excellent introduction to the desert tradition of Christian spirituality.

☐ Basil Pennington O.S.C.O, *Centering Prayer*, Doubleday, 1980

Pennington expounds the mantric tradition of prayer in a way that makes it intelligible to people of differing spiritual traditions.

☐ Joan Puls, *Every Bush is Burning*, World Council of Churches, 1987

This refreshing book enables us to see that the Christian concept of the 'kingdom of God' means in the routine of our everyday life.

☐ Herbert Slade, *Exploration into Contemplative Prayer*, Darton, Longman and Todd, 1975

Slade gives an in-depth experiential account of the tradition of contemplative prayer, drawing on the centuries of accumulated wisdom of those who journeyed well with the Cosmic Lover.

☐ Rayner Torkington, *Peter Calvey — Hermit*, Spectrum, 1977

☐ Rayner Torkington, *Peter Calvey — Prophet*, Spenithorne, 1987

These two books present fascinating stories set in the Outer Hebrides. A person in search of meaning in the life of prayer encounters Peter, a hermit, who gives him considerable assistance. The style of writing disarmingly has the feel of a novel in which profound truths are presented.

☐ Simon Tugwell, *Prayer (Volume 1) — Living with God*, Veritas, 1974

☐ Simon Tugwell, *Prayer (Volume 2) — Prayer in Practice*, Veritas, 1974

These two books give an excellent overview of the life of prayer in the best Western tradition.

☐ Ann and Barry Ulanov, *Primary Speech*, John Knox Press, 1982

This is a seminal work on the psychology of prayer. The writers assert rightly that everybody prays and people pray whether or not they call it prayer. I found this particularly helpful in understanding a little of what people experience when they pray. It is particularly helpful for those who find themselves being asked to guide others on the journey.

☐ Neville Ward, *The Use of Praying*, Epworth, 1968

This book has been a help to so many that it rightly deserves the title of 'contemporary classic'.

☐ Olive Wyon, *Prayer*, Collins Fontana, 1962

Now over thirty years since it was written and not widely available today, it is worth begging for or borrowing a copy (if not stealing one!). Olive Wyon has written simply yet profoundly on the meaning of prayer, asking and discussing such questions as why we pray and how prayer works.